I Hike Again

Also from Lawton Grinter

I Hike: Mostly True Stories from 10,000 Miles of Hiking

I Hike Again

Mostly True Stories from 15,000 Miles of Hiking

Lawton Grinter

Grand Mesa Press

Salida, Colorado

FIRST PAPERBACK EDITION

Grinter, Lawton.

I hike again : mostly true stories from 15,000 miles of hiking / by Lawton Grinter.

Published by Grand Mesa Press, P.O. Box 255, Salida, Colorado 81201 info@grandmesapress.com

Cover photo: Felicia Hermosillo
Cover design: Leslie Henslee
Copy editor: Barbara Grinter

ISBN (paperback): 978-0-9852415-2-0
ISBN (ebook): 978-0-9852415-3-7

Library of Congress Control Number: 2019900978

Library of Congress subject headings:

1. Hiking—United States—Biography. 2. Adventure and adventurers—United States—Biography. 3. Appalachian Trail—Description and travel. 4. Pacific Crest Trail—Description and travel. 5. Continental Divide Trail—Description and travel. 6. Arizona Trail—Description and travel. 7. Te Araroa—Description and travel. 8. Grinter, Lawton—1976—Travel. I. Title.

For P.O.D.

~ Contents ~

~ Foreword ~

Mother Nature has a happy knack for putting life into perspective. And those who walk in the woods on a regular basis understand this better than most. A long-distance rambler by the name of "Bo" once described the phenomena as follows:

At some point everything comes more into focus: colors become more vivid, food tastes better, jokes are funnier, the scenery becomes more amazing, and injuries become less painful. When in this state, the world makes sense to me, and I feel connected to everything around me, and grateful. I suppose others call this being in the "moment." I suspect that endorphins play a part in this change, as does the fresh air, exercise, sleep, etc. Whatever the explanation, it is indescribable to those of you that have not experienced it.

One man who intimately relates to this heightened sense of unity and appreciation is the author of *I Hike Again*, Lawton "Disco" Grinter. Through his day job as a forester and his moonlighting gig (or is it the other way around?) as a backpacking wordsmith, Disco lights up quicker than a hippy at a *Grateful Dead* concert when he starts waxing lyrical about the wilderness. The guy simply loves being out there, and sharing that passion for all things hiking is really what this book is all about.

From his earliest days as a wide-eyed kid on an Outward Bound course to some of his more recent excursions on the hydrationally-challenged Grand Enchantment and Hayduke Trails, Disco's 15,000 mile hiking journey has seen more than its fair share of ups and downs. Yet through the frequent topographical highs and the occasional emotional lows, you always get the distinct feeling that, no matter what happens to the boy from Gaffney, South Carolina, there will always be another hiking trip just around the corner. He is what I like to call a "backcountry lifer" - someone who, irrespective of the conditions or environment, will always find a way to keep heading out into the boonies.

Besides his unconditional love for spending time in the natural world, the other thing that stands out for me when reading Disco's vignettes are the colorful characters. His stories shine a headlamp on the endearingly quirky and sometimes flat-out crazy folks that to no small degree make up the US long-distance hiking world. During my years of rambling on America's mega-trails, I have met more than a few of these personalities myself. Some of the more memorable have included the taser-zapping boys of Reliance, Tennessee, an elderly English gentleman who happily went by the trail name of "Teabag" (he enjoyed a Twinings with every meal), and a mustachioed fellow by the name of "Train" (wedding, rather than choo-choo), who hiked the entire 2,660 miles of the Pacific Crest Trail in a series of bridal gowns (26 in total; one for every 100 miles). But of all the eccentrics I've encountered during my time hiking in the States, perhaps the wackiest of them all was a man called Duane. Insane Duane.

Hailing from the swamps of Florida, Duane was 49 years young when we met on the Pacific Crest Trail in 2012. It was an overcast morning about 40 miles south of Ashland, Oregon, and I was sitting on a log at the edge of a snowbank, enjoying a late breakfast of granola with powdered milk. As I munched and crunched away, I was approached by a fast-moving, long-haired, wild-looking guy, who was wearing a ragged dress shirt that had a huge rip in the left arm.

"Hey," I said.

"Are you Swami?" he replied, in a barely decipherable southern (maybe) accent without the hint of a smile.

The guy had a *Shining*-esque stare and was more weather-beaten than a Tasmanian lighthouse, so I paused for a long second before finally answering, "yes."

"My name is Insane Duane. I've been trying to catch you for 1,400 miles," the man offered.

Jesus.

This meeting between stalker and unsuspecting prey began an unlikely on-and-off-again hiking partnership that would last until the US/Canadian border. During our time together Duane regaled me with tales from his ten-year stretch in a Florida prison, the relationship he formed with a 74-year-old widower whom he met while working part-time at an old-folks home after being released from jail, and the ins and outs of living off the grid in the swamp - think canoes, hammocks, gators, bugs and bush tucker. Other fun facts about my mate Duane: 1. At the time of our meeting in 2012 he had never owned a computer or had a credit card; 2. Due to the fact he had no navigation skills whatsoever, he regularly carried an extra day or two of food because he got lost so frequently; 3. He was the biggest tipper I have ever met and always had a thick wad of $100 bills in his wallet. When I asked him about the source of his wealth, he replied, "pre-prison savings"; 4. Despite carrying a heavyish pack (base weight of approximately 15 pounds), he was one of the fastest and strongest hikers I have ever met. The guy was indefatigable. During his decade in the clink, Duane had made himself harder than a coffin nail through a regimen of endless pushups, sit-ups, pull-ups, and running (both in the prison yard as well as on the spot in his cell). When I asked him how he became interested in long-distance hiking, he replied, "In prison I read an article about the Appalachian Trail in a *National Geographic* magazine. After all those years of being locked up, I liked the idea of spending time out in nature. And moving from A to B rather than round in circles definitely had its appeal as well."

Duane and I (along with Matt "Mouse" Zion) were the first people to finish the PCT in 2012 (July 29). I haven't heard from him in the years since, but I'd like to think he is still plying the swamps of Florida in his canoe, as well as making the occasional excursion on America's long-distance trails. He was a true original and, if it weren't for hiking, I would have never met the guy. And that bringing together of disparate souls is one of the things I love most about trail life. In the woods it doesn't matter (or at least it shouldn't matter) how old you are, what you look like, where you are from, or what you do for a living. Mother Nature's welcome mat is always out. All you really need is a pack, a pair of running shoes and the desire to, in the words of Mr. Grinter himself, "get on the trail!" Hope to see a few of you out there (Note: Non-stalkers only).

Cam "Swami" Honan
Long-Distance Hiker
TheHikingLife.com

~ Author's Introduction ~

In the introduction to my first book, *I Hike*, I threatened to write another book upon the completion of another 10,000 miles of hiking. Well, I haven't quite hiked another 10,000 miles, but I did write another book. My apologies.

I Hike Again is a bit broader in scope, covering new trails and trails outside these here United States. A lot of the blame for hiking these new trails can be placed squarely on the *The Trail Show* podcast that I co-host with four like-minded individuals (read reprobates).

We started *The Trail Show* back in 2012 shortly after the publication of *I Hike*. On each month's show we feature a different trail in the "Trail of the Month" segment. Many of our guests have done quite the sales job in making many of these trails sound irresistible.

My friend Eric Payne sold me on hiking the Grand Enchantment Trail after guesting on the show and showing me all the incredible photos he took while thru-hiking the GET. Shortly thereafter in March 2014 I found myself on the outskirts of Phoenix with another reprobate named Skittles, hiking to Albuquerque over the course of 800 miles and six weeks.

A subsequent guest on *The Trail Show* (who will never again be trusted for trail advice) led my wife, P.O.D., and me to sell our house in Denver, fly to New Zealand and hike the 2,000 mile Te Araroa trail over the course of four months. Te Araroa wasn't quite what we expected and differed significantly from what our friend had described. He has received pallets of hate mail from us ever since, but we've mostly forgiven him at this point (mostly).

Reflecting on what a great hike the Grand Enchantment Trail had been, I found myself wanting to do more hiking in the desert southwest. That, coupled with *The Trail Show* episode we did on the Arizona Trail, led me down to southern Arizona in the spring of 2017. I had only a month and was able to hike close to 600 miles from the Mexican border to Flagstaff.

Skittles had some free time on his hands that autumn so we picked up where I had left off in Flagstaff. We hiked north through the Grand Canyon to the Utah border and beyond into Buckskin Gulch and Paria Canyon. I had never set foot in the Grand Canyon before and that hike left me spellbound. Paria Canyon was the icing on the cake.

I almost forgot the failed hike P.O.D. and I did in the Pyrenees of Spain in 2012. You'll read about it shortly. Don't go hiking in Spain in August. It's hot. You will hate yourself.

I guess they can't all be zingers. Even the hikes that turn out to be not quite what I was looking for leave a lasting impression. Misery has a way of doing that I suppose. And then some time passes and the bad times are forgotten and the good times are magnified and then another hike is planned. One hike leads to another and another and, before you know it, you've walked 15,000 miles.

So why hike? Why head out into the unknown to face all sorts of adversity and trouble? Why leave the comfort of a cozy home and a steady paycheck to wander into a godforsaken place that most of your friends and family would find foreboding at best? These are all good questions with a variety of answers that are vague or hard to put into words.

When asked why he wanted to climb Mt. Everest, George Mallory said, "Because it's there." And I suppose that is part of the reason people hike 2,000 mile trails.... because they are there. But the truth is that for some of us being out there is home. Muir said, "Going to the mountains is going home." I agree. I, too, feel most grounded and right with the world when I'm out walking a trail in the tall woods.

When people ask me why I hike, I typically ask them what their favorite sport is. Golf. "You feel the same way about golf that I do about walking long trails," I typically offer. Usually they "get it" after I give them this analogy, although, most of them can't fathom hiking 2,000 miles in one clip. Sometimes I can't either.

I also feel that any one of us may be really good at or have a natural aptitude for a multitude of physical pursuits, but only if we are lucky enough to be introduced to said sport. You could be one of the most incredible Jai Lai players ever to set foot on a concha, but unless you actually play Jai Lai you will likely never know. For me, I was lucky enough to have been introduced to long-distance hiking over 20 years ago by my friend Jake. Turns out that I'm pretty good at it. I guess that's why I keep doing it. That and it beats working the 9 to 5 any day of the week.

~~~

As with my first book, this book's contents jump around in place and time over the course of 25+ years of long and short hikes on a multitude of trails around the globe. The stories aren't chronological but they are memorable, which is why they're in this book.

All of the people and places in this book are or were real. I changed a few names here and there to protect both the innocent and the guilty. I'm sure they won't mind and I hope you won't either.

Enjoy.

Lawton "Disco" Grinter
January 2019
The Victoria Tavern
Salida, Colorado

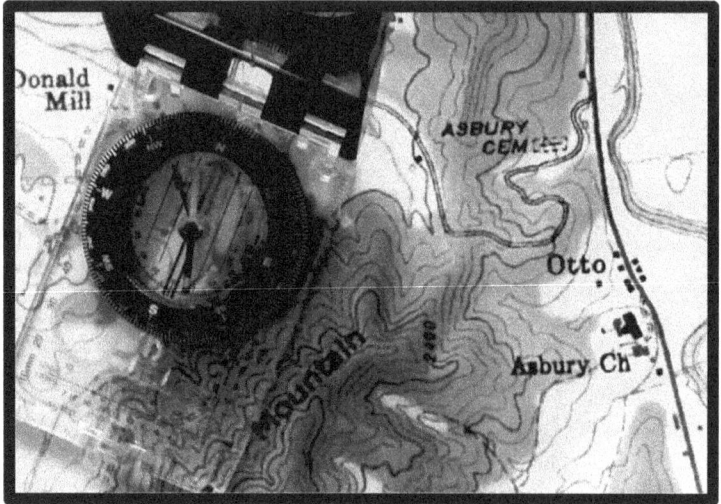

1

Outward Bound

66 **I**'m not interested in going to basketball camp. I'd rather go to a wilderness camp," I said to my mom as we drove towards Food Lion.

"You don't want to go to basketball camp? You always had fun at basketball camp," my mom implored.

I stared out the window and thought about how quickly I wanted to leave after I had arrived at the Dean Smith Basketball School the previous summer. My desire to shoot hoops had waned in the middle of my teenage years. I was looking for something different. Something new. Something challenging.

"I think the Hartzog's son went to an outdoor camp a few summers ago. I'll check with Will to see where it was. Outbound or Outward something is what she called it," my mom replied.

A few days later my mom told me the "camp" her friend's son went to was called Outward Bound.

"He did lots of different things: hiking, rock climbing, wilderness skills and map reading," she relayed as I imagined myself doing those exact same things.

I'd been playing out in the woods behind my grandma's house for as long as I could remember. My grandma would pick me up every day from elementary school and I'd get an hour of pure freedom to run wild in those woods. The neighborhood kids and I would build forts, run through the streams, play hide and seek and run full speed into any and all activities that ended up in dirty jeans and a sweat-soaked shirt.

Being in the woods was second nature by the time I hit my teenage years. I spent a lot of time on a skateboard and moonlighted as a basketball player here and there, but my true passion was the forest.

"Sign me up," I told my mom as I was winding down my last year of junior high school with an eye towards the summer.

~~~

Four months later I found myself in Asheville, North Carolina. My dad had come up from Alabama and my mom and sister had driven me the two and a half hours from my hometown of Gaffney, South Carolina, to get there. It was August and my 16-day Outward Bound course would start the following day.

There were anxious teenagers and even more anxious parents scurrying about the pre-arranged meeting location to kickoff the adventure. I was really looking forward to a nice relaxing summer camp in the woods. There'd be archery, games, a day hike or two and maybe boat races. We'd catch butterflies, go fishing and roast marshmallows by campfire at night. I said my goodbyes to my family and watched them drive off into the afternoon. I climbed onto a waiting bus to be taken to the Outward Bound basecamp.

"My brother's friend said Outward Bound was the hardest thing he's ever done," the kid with braces in the seat in front of me said as we hurtled down the highway.

"Yeah, it's supposed to be really hard. I just got out of "juvie" and my dad told me if I didn't finish the course he'd send me back," the lanky looking stoner beside me replied.

Hmmm. I looked out the dirty glass window and began to wonder what I had signed up for. "Hardest thing he's ever done".... "juvie".... surely they were mistaken. This was just a pleasant camp in the woods for two weeks.

I closed my eyes and tried to catch a quick nap. I had no idea what my bus mates were talking about. I decided it wasn't worth worrying over and all would be revealed soon enough.

We piled off the charter buses and were organized into groups of twelve. All told there were eight groups of twelve and all of us were directed to a meadow where a guy with a big beard and reading glasses told us that we were in for two weeks of shared adventure and outdoor challenges. "The goal is deeper understanding of oneself, one's fellow humans, and life itself," he offered as we stared wide-eyed back at him with nary a clue.

Then we commenced to play a game in the meadow, which was a modified version of freeze tag. I think it was supposed to be an icebreaker and a chance for us to expend some energy before we started the course in earnest.

We divided back into our groups of twelve and were introduced to our camp counselors. "Jimmy Bob" and "Jay Bob" looked like roadies for *Jethro Tull*. Jimmy Bob had long brown hair gathered into a ponytail that draped halfway down his back, and Jay Bob had longish curly hair reminiscent of Alfred Matthew Yankovic also known as "Weird Al" to those of us who grew up in the 80's.

Each of us was issued a drab green army rucksack and told to put the mandatory gear we brought into said rucksack. My mom and I had spent the better part of a month ordering polypropylene long johns and hiking boots out of a Cabela's catalog to check off all of the essential items on Outward Bound's "to bring" list. I had no idea why I'd need polypropylene long johns or how I would fix the flashlight I brought that had already stopped working.

We packed up and walked about 15 minutes to an area where our group of 12 would base out of the next 16 days. I looked around and saw nothing but trees. No cabins. No bunkhouse. No shower house. No cafeteria. No nothing. There were two long logs that had been braced not to roll backwards. Those were our seats. The twelve of us threw down our packs and took a seat.

"How many of you were forced to come here by your parents?" Jay Bob asked the group. Ten hands went up. I looked around and noticed only one other guy besides me had not raised his hand. I immediately got a knot in my stomach. What had I just signed up for? Why were ten of my campmates sent here against their wills?

Jimmy Bob and Jay Bob split up the shared gear and informed us we'd be sleeping sardine style under a large tarp. They proceeded to set up our group tarp and show us the finer points of various knots we'd need to know including the taut-line hitch (a knot I still use to this day). We each were issued a half inch thick blue foam pad and a sleeping bag and told from here on out it would be on us to set up the tarp each night.

They showed us how to operate the somewhat ancient looking and well-used Primus brand stoves that our group would be sharing. They cooked our first meal of pasta as the sun slowly dropped below the trees and day turned to night. We each were given a length of parachute cord, a compass, a whistle and a knife and told to make a lanyard to hang around our necks. These would be essential items for our 16 days in the woods.

After dinner I helped clean the crusty pots with water we had trucked up from a nearby stream. A few moments later I ducked under the tarp and crawled into my sleeping bag. I wedged in between two complete strangers. I couldn't remember their names, but both had raised their hands earlier that evening. I wondered what they had done to be forced to come here by their parents. My watch said 8:30 p.m. I hadn't gone to bed this early in years.

~~~

Day two dawned bright and early. Jimmy Bob and Jay Bob rousted us just after 6 a.m. We scarfed down a breakfast of bagels, cream cheese and cold water. The 12 of us were led down to a ropes course near the previous day's meadow and given helmets and climbing harnesses. The day would be spent traversing steel cables 50 feet above the ground. We learned the crucial details of clipping on and off of the cables and the verbal commands required before heading out on the wire. I went from being very excited to slightly terrified as I was encouraged to try to walk the wire like a tight rope without using my hands. They wanted us to trust the carabiners, climbing harnesses, and other gear that secured us safely to a lead wire above us while the only thing I could see were the small frames of Jimmy Bob and Jay Bob on the ground some 50 feet below.

I had never been on a ropes course before. I had never camped under a tarp before. I had never even had a bagel. I grew up in the land of biscuits and gravy. Bagels were something northerners ate. These two weeks were going to be different. A departure from the norm. Little did I know these two weeks would change the direction of my life. Little did I know I'd be a different person on a different path just 16 short days later.

Back at camp that afternoon one of my campmates, Kevin, asked Jimmy Bob when we'd get to shower. Jimmy Bob stared blankly back at Kevin. I'd seen the same look from the lady at the DMV when I asked her if I could take my Driver's License photo again because I blinked. Jim Bob gave some long and obscure diatribe about how humans existed for millennia without showers and that soap was unnecessary to be clean. He told us that gallons of precious water were wasted while showering and how Americans use eight times as much water per day as people living in third world countries.

"You'll adapt and be better for it," he assured Kevin as he walked away. Kevin and I stared blankly at Jimmy Bob and then blankly at each other. I think I had skipped one day without a shower or a bath before. Possibly two days. But definitely nothing more than that. No way. I shrugged it off and assumed Jimmy Bob was bluffing. We'd get showers in the next day or so.

~ ~ ~

Our group boarded a large unmarked passenger van the next morning and rumbled down a dirt road towards a distant trailhead. The plan was to spend three days backpacking in the Appalachian Mountains. Our dirty dozen of 15-year-olds headed into the wilderness led by the valiant Jimmy and Jay Bob. A third adult joined us. Yuri was half Russian, half Polish, and a heck of a rock climber. He didn't like the little raised button that sits atop most ball caps so he ripped the button off his cap in front of us at our first break.

Jimmy Bob informed us that we would be hiking 30 miles of trail over three days and we'd see all kinds of terrain: steep rocky cliffs, dense forest, meadows and everything in between. He casually mentioned he hoped we'd have a chance to camp on a slope. I wasn't sure what he meant as I had no frame of reference having never backpacked before.

We hiked into the night to get our ten miles completed and camped at a spot that Jim Bob had in mind. The adults never camped directly with us. They always picked a spot 30 or so yards away. I was never quite sure why until I spied Jay Bob blowing up an inflatable sleeping pad one night. There would be mutiny if those of us on the thin foam mats knew our counselors were spending comfortable nights of luxury on thick inflatable mattresses!

We fiddled around with the knots needed to guy out our tarp. The camping area the Bobs picked did seem a bit sloped. Actually, as I stepped back, I estimated the area under the tarp to be at 25 degrees or so. I was too exhausted from the day's hike to care. And my shoulders were killing me from the rucksack. Overhiked and underslept. Need to shut eyes....

The sun hit my face bright and early through a break in the trees. As I came out of a deep sleep I couldn't figure out where the tarp was. I sat up and looked directly at the tree above me and then around to see a forest floor of crunchy oak leaves from the previous autumn that had yet to decay. I turned around and looked up above my head and behind me to where the tarp was located. I had slid completely down the hill, out from under the tarp and off my sleeping pad, and somehow managed to stay asleep!

The night before a skinny kid named Tim had been crying a low cry to himself under the tarp. Kevin told me that Tim was homesick. Most nights for the rest of the trip we'd hear Tim sniffling a bit under the tarp as we were going to sleep. I don't think that Tim had ever been away from the comforts of his Florida home. And I feel certain that he, too, had never eaten a bagel before because at our first break, he began choking on an all too large piece of unchewed bagel stuck in his windpipe. Everyone freaked out. Everyone but Yuri.

I've taken various CPR and First Aid courses over the years and have listened to many a lecture about what to do when someone is choking. I've seen illustrations of the Heimlich Maneuver.... they always show the chokers as red faced and grasping their own necks with both hands. Tim was a carbon copy of the drawing in my first aid book. He immediately stood up and grabbed his neck with both hands, while his face turned red with tears streaming from his eyes. He looked absolutely panicked. Yuri hustled over, got behind him and did two short but powerful abdominal thrusts. On the second thrust I watched a piece of bagel the size of a doughnut hole arc across the North Carolina sky and land about five feet from Tim's shoe.

We were all thunderstruck and dead quiet. It's not everyday that you watch someone save a life. Tim was really shaken up and in tears. He thanked Yuri profusely for saving his life. Yuri told him to think nothing of it. Within five minutes Tim was done crying and hungry again. He finished eating the bagel and on we hiked.

~~~

We completed the three-day backpack and two days of rock climbing. It was now evident that we, in fact, were not getting showers. Jimmy Bob wasn't bluffing. The closest I had gotten to clean was splashing ice-cold water onto my face from the infrequent streams we crossed. When we got back to basecamp after our rock climbing foray, there was a very brief ten minutes when Jimmy and Jay Bob had to leave our group and go meet with their boss.

There had been two guys in particular that had been talking back and giving the Bobs much grief. Kyle and Justin were troublemakers and I had befriended them early in the trip. The three of us gathered by the side of our basecamp area and I told them about the cinder block building with bathrooms I had seen down near the meadow where we had all played the game of freeze tag during that first afternoon.

16

"I saw a Men's and Women's sign on two different doors. Those are bathrooms guys. I bet there's running water.... hot water. Follow me," I said in the hushed tones normally used when whispering something to a friend during Sunday services.

I knew we had to be quick. We hustled at something just less than a run until we got down the hill and hit the dirt road by the cinder block building. The three of us peered around, saw no one, and then casually walked into the men's bathroom as if we owned the place. Two sinks with running water and bar soap. The right faucet had an "H" on it. For the next 60 glorious seconds I washed my hands and face with hot water and a cracked piece of grimy bar soap. 60 seconds of heavenly bliss. I watched the sink run brown with filth and grime. I looked into the mirror and saw my reflection for the first time in a week. And then I casually walked out of the Outward Bound basecamp staff bathroom and scurried back up the hill. Kyle and Justin had done the same thing and were right behind me. Jimmy and Jay Bob showed up a minute later and were none the wiser. Our first rebellion had gone off without a hitch. We were emboldened.

~~~

Heading into our second week of Outward Bound we were told to get ready for a four-day backpack. We loaded our gear and enough food to last four days and piled into the unmarked passenger van once again. It was a hot day and the smell of twelve unwashed 15-year-olds in a van with no air conditioning was apparent. This would be a

36-mile hike, most of which would be on the famed Appalachian Trail.

Our 36-mile hike would take us by the Albert Mountain fire tower and across the Georgia/North Carolina border. The hiking was tough and our crew was worn down after having logged a week of difficult adventures coupled with the haggard sleep one gets when lying prone on a half-inch thick foam pad. Jimmy Bob talked to us during our first lunch break about the Appalachian Trail. He explained that this trail actually goes much further than just the 36 miles we were on. It actually went all the way to Maine.

I didn't exactly know where Maine was, but I did know it would probably take a long car drive to get there. Jimmy Bob told us the entire trail was over 2,000 miles long. That's an impossible distance for a 15-year-old to comprehend. I remembered the Appalachian Trail sign attached to the bridge over the Nantahala River. My dad and I had been rafting that river together every summer since I was eight or nine. It was one of my dad's favorite rivers and had become one of mine. I was able to grasp that the piece of trail I was standing on somehow connected to the bridge over the Nantahala River. Pretty cool.

By our third day on the AT, Kyle had been mouthing off more than usual to Jimmy and Jay Bob. At some point in the late afternoon we took a break and to mess with the Bobs a bit more, Kyle refused to go on. He wouldn't put his backpack on and he wouldn't stand up. He sat crumpled on the side of the trail with his arms crossed and a scowl on his face.

"I'm not going anywhere. I'm done with this hike," he yelled at Jay Bob who was standing in front of him.

Jay Bob explained that he was holding up the entire group and that he had to keep going.

"We are in the middle of the woods on a trail. Nobody is coming out here to take you home. Let's go. It's time to put on your backpack and get moving. The longer you wait here, the longer we have to hike tonight," Jay said, trying to rationalize with an irrational teenager.

Kyle grudgingly got up and uttered a few threats and cuss words. He put on his pack and hiked with the rest of us for the next 20 minutes. And then he stopped. He threw his pack down and once again said he wasn't going any further.

What happened next was unexpected, shocking and slightly horrendous. Kyle was in the back of our group and luckily I was towards the front so my initial view of him pulling his pants down and squatting in the middle of the trail was a bit obscured. By the time he proceeded to release his bowels on the middle of the trail almost all of our crew was at a full run to get away from the situation.

The kid had pulled his pants down and taken a dump right in the middle of the Appalachian Trail in full view of

Jimmy Bob and Jay Bob (who were hiking up behind him) to mount a protest the likes of which the North Carolina Outward Bound School had never seen. I can't imagine what was going through Kyle's mind when he did this. And I can't imagine what Jimmy and Jay Bob were thinking when they saw him do this.

We heard some loud angry talking between the Bobs and Kyle. Our group was a few minutes ahead at this point and out of view of the entire scene. Jay Bob hurried up to us and told us to wait on them until they got everything sorted out.

A long half-hour later Kyle and the Bobs finally walked up to us. Kyle was silent and the Bobs informed us we'd now be hiking well past dark in order to get to our evening's destination. At some point later that evening Justin relayed to me that the Bobs made Kyle go dig a hole off trail and transport via a large flat rock the sullied contents he had released onto the Appalachian Trail to said hole. Kyle had initially refused to do this, but the Bobs told him they would stay there all night if they had to and wouldn't go any further until he cleaned up his mess. Eventually Kyle relented and we hiked into the night.

Although this incident really threw the group (and the Bobs) for a loop, one good thing did come out of our 36-mile hike along the AT. When we started the hike, Jimmy and Jay Bob explained that all the navigating would be left up to us. They showed us our starting point and our ending point on a USGS topo map and explained the finer points of navigating with a map and compass. Staying on the AT is usually fairly easy as it's typically well-marked, well-maintained and an obvious footpath, but the last five miles of our hike would involve branching off on a series of side trails to get to a remote trailhead where our passenger van would be waiting.

They explained that the double dashed lines were four wheel drive roads and that the single dashed lines were hiking trails. The little black rectangles were buildings along the thicker solid lines that represented highways. We practiced orienting our compasses north and then rotating the map so that it too was facing north. We discussed the contour lines on the map and were told that they represented 40 feet of elevation change. By day two we had all become pretty good at using our map and compass to approximate where we were and how far we had gone.... and how steep the upcoming climbs would be.

When it came time to branch off the AT onto the series of side trails, we didn't miss a beat. Our group was a fine-tuned navigating machine. We popped out of the woods late in the afternoon on day four to a passenger van driven by our rock climbing, Heimlich Maneuvering hero, Yuri.

On the ride back to basecamp we were told that the following day would be a day of service doing stream restoration. And then we were told the two days after that would be the grand finale.... 48 hours solo.

~ ~ ~

Each of us was issued a small personal sized tarp and enough food to last two full days. We loaded into the vans once again and headed to a trailhead on the edge of Pisgah National Forest. After an hour hiking into an area with a stream, the Bobs explained that each of us would be camping by ourselves and that this would be a time of reflection. They encouraged us to slow down our minds, meditate, and think on the week and a half that had just gone by. They gave us each a sheet of questions to try to answer in our small Outward Bound notebooks. They walked each of us to individual campsites approximately 400 yards apart along the stream. We were out of view from each other and the Bobs, but they assured us that if anything happened, we could just blow our whistle and they'd come to see what was going on.

My first 24 hours of solo were rather mundane. I tried answering a number of the questions from the sheet but became rather bored rather quickly. There was nothing to do. We weren't hiking, we weren't rock climbing, we weren't restoring streams and we weren't sneaking down to the staff bathroom to wash our faces.

I stared at the stream. I stared at the trees. And then I stared at the dirt. Birds were singing their songs and squirrels were rustling about in the dried leaves below a nearby pine. There were some inspirational quotes in my Outward Bound notebook. I read those too many times to count. I was even too bored to sleep and I had never slept by myself in the woods so it was a long night and I was glad to finally see the first rays of dawn.

By 9 a.m. I was losing my mind as I couldn't fathom how I was going to make it through another day with nothing to do. We wouldn't be done with solo for another 24 hours and I was at a loss on how to entertain myself for the rest of the day. It was then that Kyle and Justin slipped quietly into my campsite.

We had been told to avoid contacting other folks in our group during solo. We had been told to spend the time reflecting and meditating. But we were 15-year-old sugar-deprived delinquents and were itching to do something.... anything that would pass the time and make our stint in the woods less miserable.

Kyle, Justin and I laid out the USGS topo map on the dirt in front of my tarp. Kyle had paid close attention to various road signs on the drive into the trailhead we had hiked in from the day before. He had taken mental notes of bends in the road and our direction of travel. He pointed to a blue line on the map representing the stream that we were now huddled by. He knew exactly where we were. My boring day in the woods had just become a lot more interesting.

I pointed to the double dashed line approximately three quarters of a mile north of our stream. That line extended roughly two miles to a solid line that appeared to be a highway. And that solid line headed east five miles to an intersection with another highway that contained more than a few little black rectangles.... buildings! The name "Otto" was written on the map where these buildings were congregated.

Otto, North Carolina, is a very small community spread out along Highway 23 just north of the Georgia border and just south of the town of Franklin. It has a volunteer fire department, post office, a few residences and a convenience store. It would only take the three of us just over an hour to get there.

After examining the map in detail and using our newfound navigational skills, we determined that we were approximately 7-8 miles all told from Otto. It was mid-morning and, with nothing else to do for the rest of the day, we decided to hike to Otto to try to buy some soda and candy. We thought maybe, just maybe, there'd be a 7-Eleven there filled with cold sodas and sugary treats. Sugar is eight times more addictive than cocaine and after 10+ days with no junk food, it's all that our 15-year-old minds could think about. Our addiction could only be cured with candy.... lots of candy. With that we very quietly glided out the back of my campsite and disappeared into the woods heading north.

30 minutes later we reached our double dashed line on the map. What was supposed to be just a four wheel drive road turned out to be a graded dirt road with houses located sporadically along its edge. Within 10 minutes an old fellow in an even older Ford pickup truck pulled along side us and asked what we were doing. We made up some story about being on vacation with our family and had

gotten bored and were heading into town. The old guy said he was headed to the post office and agreed to give us a ride. We piled in and got driven straight into town. Just down the highway from the post office I spied a building with a couple of gas pumps out front and an RC Cola sign. Bingo!

We casually walked into the slightly run-down convenience store on the side of Highway 23. I saw the standard beef jerky and jar of pickled pigs feet by the register. Four glass doors at the back of the store enclosed every ice cold drink we could possibly have hoped for. As I rounded the corner of the middle isle, I thought I heard the faint sounds of heavenly harp music. There before me lay 15 feet and three shelves full of every candy known to man. Lemonheads, Starburst, Tootsie Rolls, Cherry Clan, Alexander the Grape, Kit Kat bars, Snickers, Twix, Watchamacallit, Blow Pops, Bubbaliscious, Reese's Pieces, ad infinitum.

Kyle, Justin and I stared at all the possibilities for a couple of minutes without saying a word.

"How much money do you guys have?" I asked.

Both of them reached into their pockets and pulled out nothing but their stashed Outward Bound p-cord lanyards with compass, whistle and knife. I shook my head. I had a $20 bill that my dad had given me for "incidentals." Little did either of us know that there would be nowhere to spend money at Outward Bound.

That is unless, of course, you bailed on your 48 hours of solo and hitched into Otto, North Carolina.

"That'll be $19.78," the man behind the counter said. "Would you like a bag?"

"Yes please. Thanks," I replied as he bagged up a delicious array of artificially sweetened junk food and pushed it across the counter to me.

Kyle, Justin and I walked out the door and around the side of the building to a picnic table. The three of us spent the next 20 minutes gobbling candy with reckless abandon. We were two-thirds of the way through the bag when Justin suggested we save some for camp. The thought of stopping our candy binge had not occurred to Kyle and me but, after much discussion, it made sense. We divided up the rest of the bag among the three of us. A glance of my watch said 1:00 p.m. We now had to get the eight miles back to our solo campsites along the creek.

A planning session ensued. We felt we could walk the series of roads back to camp and be there in about three hours. But we didn't want to walk. It had been so easy getting a ride to town. Surely we could get a ride back to the dirt road where the old man had picked us up. We'd thumb it and get up there fast.

We chose a spot in the shade just up the main paved road that would lead five miles to our dirt road. We stuck our thumbs out and watched as car after car drove by. 10 minutes went by, then 30, then an hour. Ugh. This was not going so well. At this point it was after two o'clock and we were beginning to think we may need to just walk the road shoulder all the way back. We stuck our thumbs out one last time as a small truck with a camper top pulled over. The glass on the camper top was covered in stickers. A few of those were North Carolina Outward Bound School stickers.

Kyle looked at Justin and me and said, "Be cool. I'll go talk to him." Kyle walked over to the passenger side door and the driver rolled down the window. We would later find out that the driver was the basecamp cook for the Outward Bound staff! We had never seen him before and lucky for us he had never seen us. He asked Kyle if we were Outward Bound students and Kyle assured him we were not and that we were on vacation with our families and needed a ride back up to our vacation home. Kyle looked back at us and told us to hop in the back of the truck. He bravely rode up front with the driver.

Right at the intersection of our paved road with the dirt road that led back towards our solo camp the truck pulled over on the road shoulder. Kyle told the driver our vacation house was just up the road and he didn't want the driver to have to go out of his way to take us all the way up there and the driver agreed. We all piled out of the truck, waved goodbye to the Outward Bound cook, and commenced walking back up our dirt road. The three of us waited a few minutes before we said a word.

"Good God," Kyle finally exclaimed! "I almost shit my pants in there!!" He stopped, bent over and put his hands on his knees, staring at the ground, exasperated.

"That guy grilled me about Outward Bound. He was certain we were Outward Bound students. I spent the entire ride playing dumb and convincing him I knew nothing about Outward Bound and that we were just on family vacation. I think he believed me," Kyle suggested, somewhat unsure.

The three of us walked the two miles up the road to the spot where we had popped out of the woods earlier that morning. It was getting toward late afternoon and the chorus of birds we had heard that morning had been replaced by silence. No one was around so we ducked back in the trees and headed south towards the stream and our solo campsites. As we got within view of my campsite we paused to discuss the plan.

"I think we're fine," Kyle said assuringly. "If Jimmy Bob or Jay Bob ask any of us where we've been, just tell them we were out exploring in the woods. Plausible deniability." What teenager uses the term "plausible deniability" I thought to myself.

We agreed that sounded like a good plan and parted ways as we each headed back to our solo campsites. I tiptoed into mine and took a seat by my tarp. I was slightly panicked as I looked around, fully expecting the Bobs to show up with other Outward Bound staff and angry faces. They'd grill me about my whereabouts all day and inform me of how disappointed my parents would be as they'd have to send me home. There would be a full inquisition and they wouldn't relent until I broke and told them everything. I would be forced to write a letter of apology and beg forgiveness for breaking the rules and for eating all that sweet, sweet candy. I'd be told about the dangers of hitchhiking and a host of other terrible outcomes that could have happened. It would be rotten and dreadful and leave me feeling really bad about the decision I'd made to leave my solo campsite.

After an hour of sitting by my tarp ridden with anxiety and not seeing Jimmy Bob or Jay Bob or anybody, I realized that nobody was coming because nobody knew. At some point right before dark I mustered a grin as I realized that we had pulled it off. Sneaking down to the staff bathroom to wash my hands with bar soap was child's play compared to what we had just accomplished. *This* was the stuff Outward Bound teenage legends were made of.

At some point the next morning Jimmy Bob and Jay Bob showed up to say that solo was over.

"How'd it go?" they asked me.

"Fine," I said.

"Did you get a chance to answer the questions we gave you," they asked.

"I got through most of them," I answered.

And that was it. The Bobs went and corralled the rest of our group and we hiked out the two miles to a waiting passenger van. Periodically Kyle and Justin would shoot a glance and a grin at me. They knew what I knew and what no one else knew.

After we arrived back at basecamp the three of us filed to the back of the line and a quick conversation ensued.

"The cook is here somewhere and he will recognize me if he sees me. If you guys see any Outward Bound staff, turn away and don't let them get a good look at your face. And don't tell anybody about what we did," Kyle whispered.

The next day Kyle and Justin were kicked out of the North Carolina Outward Bound School and sent home one day early. We only had two days left and it seemed a bit crazy to make their parents come pick them up a day early, but that's exactly what happened.

I immediately went into panic mode assuming that the Bobs had found out about our holiday in Otto.

"Hey, what happened to Kyle and Justin?" I asked Kevin who always seemed to know what was going on.

"Apparently they ran off at the mouth one too many times to Jimmy and Jay Bob. That, coupled with Kyle dropping his pants and dumping in the middle of the Appalachian Trail. And apparently Justin said something about Jimmy Bob's mother that didn't go over well," Kevin relayed.

"How'd you find out all that?" I asked, still not believing their getting kicked out had nothing to do with our hitchhiking.

"I overheard Jimmy and Jay Bob talking right before lunch," Kevin said matter of factly.

It happened so fast. Kyle and Justin were gathering their belongings before any of us even knew what was taking place. We were all told to stay put as the Bobs marched Kyle and Justin down to basecamp headquarters. A few hours later their parents showed up to take them home and the Bobs were mum about it all when they came back to our group camping area.

I didn't even get a chance to say goodbye to my partners in crime. They had disappeared faster than a fart in a wind tunnel. I had skated only because I never felt compelled to mouth off at the Bobs and thankfully Kyle and Justin had told no one about our excursion. I felt a bit of survivor's guilt, but that feeling quickly disappeared as I snuck a couple of Starbursts into my mouth from my leftover stash.

2a

Baltimore Jack

"When you see Baltimore Jack tell him I said hello," Brian said to me, almost as if he were a mutual friend of mine.

"Who?" I asked, not sure I had heard the name correctly.

"Baltimore Jack. You'll run into him at some point this summer," Brian confirmed.

It was early 1999 and just a few months before I was set to start my Appalachian Trail thru-hike. Brian was a friend of a friend who had hiked most of the trail the year before. I knew nothing of trail names or the people out there who hiked trails year after year. I thought it would be pretty slim odds that I would randomly run into some guy during my hike of the AT that Brian had met the year before. There are thousands of people attempting to thru-hike the AT each year and all these folks start at different times (and even different places), and go at different paces. Heck, you could be hiking the same stretch of trail the same day as another hiker and never see them if they got up earlier than you or ducked off the trail to relieve themselves while you walked by.

What I didn't know was that the first day of spring, March 21ˢᵗ, was an immensely popular day to start an Appalachian Trail thru-hike. Apparently Baltimore Jack had the same idea I did. He was the first thru-hiker I met on the first day of my thru-hike. I told him that Brian said hello.

~~~

Every hiking season on most every trail in the United States there are a gaggle of folks trying to hike from one end to the other. All walks of life are represented, as are ages, gender, religion, you name it. Among the hearty souls that are out there trying to make their way from Georgia to Maine or Mexico to Canada, there are always a few unique characters that gain a reputation for one reason or another.

In 1999 on the Appalachian Trail there was a guy who called himself Johnny Reb. He signed all the trail registers "Johnny Reb – Journeyman for Jesus." And Johnny Reb hiked 20 miles a day every day with no days off…. ever.

The late 90's saw ultralight backpacking in its infancy. There was still a gang of external frame packs and lots of heavy leather hiking boots out there. Folks might scoff a bit at 20 miles a day now, given how light equipment is and how comfortable footwear has gotten, but I can tell you that Johnny Reb - Journeyman for Jesus - had none of that. He was carrying a heavy pack, wearing heavy boots and he had something to prove.

I never met Johnny Reb in 1999 as he was always ahead of me. He was always ahead of most everyone. There was a guy, though, named Tomcat who had started early enough that Johnny Reb was initially behind him. At some point in the first month on the trail Johnny Reb caught up with Tomcat. Tomcat was able to hang with Johnny Reb for a day or two and then he fell behind. As Johnny Reb continued to sign trail registers "Johnny Reb - Journeyman for Jesus," Tomcat began signing registers "Tomcat - Journeyman for Johnny Reb."

I always made it a point to look for Johnny Reb's trail register entries when I'd stop to take a break at one of the 250+ shelters located along the Appalachian Trail. The further north I got, the more it seemed evident that Johnny Reb - Journeyman for Jesus - needed a day off. Mentions of aches, pains, trials and tribulations were the centerpiece of his brief notations in the trail registers. I felt for Johnny Reb and I was in awe of him, too. Like clockwork he would hike 20+ miles every day and he never took a day off. I never met Johnny Reb, but I respected him.

Johnny Reb finished his 1999 Appalachian Trail thru-hike in less than 3 months. Pete Palmer (a.k.a. Cujo) finished his 1999 Appalachian Trail thru hike in less than 2 months. Much less actually. 48 days 20 hours and 11 minutes. It was a new supported speed record that year and Pete's reputation spread fast among hikers on the trail.

Pete was a mailman and ultrarunner from Connecticut. He set out on May 10th from Springer Mountain in Georgia to beat David Horton's previously set fastest known time. Word spread fast about Pete. It's amazing how someone's reputation can become so large that word about them travels in front of them! And this was the day and age when rarely anyone had a cell phone. I saw three cell phones total during the five months that I was on trail in 1999. Three.

I never met Pete Palmer either. The day he passed me (I later figured out), I was fast asleep in my tent somewhere along the trail in Maryland. I suppose I had the luxury of sleeping in and Pete did not. I made it to the northern terminus of the Appalachian Trail (Mt. Katahdin, Maine) on August 26th. Pete made it there on June 28th. Pete had started a month and a half after I did. Incredible.

The AT had a host of other well-known characters that had trod its well-worn path. You know your hiker celebrity status has reached new heights when hikers out on the trail in subsequent years are still talking about you.

Lucy and Susan Letcher, a.k.a. Isis and Jackrabbit, hiked the trail from Georgia to Maine devoid of shoes. They quickly became known as the "Barefoot Sisters." They had such a good time on that first AT hike that they decided to hike the entire trail again in the opposite direction from Maine to Georgia.... barefoot, of course. I can't imagine going through the 40+ mile section of AT known as the

"Pennsylvania Rocks" without boots, shoes, flip flops.... something!

Scott Rimm-Hewitt hiked the entire length of the AT with an 18 pound tuba. He quickly picked up the trail name "Tuba Man" and was known to serenade hikers and nearby ungulates with the sounds of his Besson 983. At some point during his thru-hike of the AT in 2000, he fell headfirst off a rocky prominence in Pennsylvania called "The Knife Edge" only to land on the tuba instead of his head. The tuba broke his fall and likely saved his life! Most hikers didn't know that Scott was also an accomplished runner. Before he set foot on the Appalachian Trail, he qualified for the Boston Marathon and decided to run it with his tuba, because that's what you do when you are known as "Super Scott the Tuba Man." He would have finished the Boston in under 5 hours but he stopped for 15 minutes to serenade a group of onlookers. And to add an exclamation point to his tuba exploits, he biked 3,000+ miles from Portland, Oregon, to Portland, Maine – with his tuba in tow.

~ ~ ~

Anyway, folks that know, or know of, Baltimore Jack will tell you he was "one of a kind." I got to know Jack fairly well that first month on the trail as he and I were hiking at roughly the same pace. He showed me a few tricks about how to resupply on the cheap, buying generic off-brand pasta, olive oil and spaghetti powder and adding your own spices. He would frequently send his maildrops to hotels or businesses along the trail as opposed to trail town post offices to avoid being hamstrung by the post office's lack of weekend business hours. I found myself hosed more than once getting to a town on a Saturday afternoon only to find the local post office that contained my maildrop wasn't opening again until Monday morning. That meant two nights in a hotel and a thinner wallet by the time I finally got my mail.

But Jack had it all dialed in, which makes sense given that 1999 was the year that Jack completed his third complete hike of the Appalachian Trail. The thing with Jack I couldn't make sense of was the non-filtered cigarettes and the ever-present bottle of *Jim Beam* that Jack always carried. Here is this guy who was hiking 2,100+ miles every year over an extremely difficult trail complete with over 450,000 feet of elevation gain and loss. And somehow he was able to do it year in and year out smoking *Camels* and drinking whiskey.

Over the course of my five months on the AT I began to learn that anything was possible out there. 20 miles a day, every day, with no breaks was possible. Hiking the entire trail in 48 days was possible. And hiking the trail year in and year out with non-filtered Camels and a bottle of Beam.... also possible. 99% of AT thru-hikers are doing something much less extreme.... mundane if you will. And the 1% that aren't are the folks that the 99% talk about.

At some point after Damascus, Virginia, I had gotten ahead of Jack. One of the last things he had told me was, "Be sure and stay at the Doyle once you get to Duncannon." I told him I would. I lied. I should say that I didn't intentionally lie, as I didn't know much about the Doyle Hotel when I was in southern Virginia making my way north. But the closer I got to Duncannon, Pennsylvania, the more horror stories I heard about the place.

The Doyle has changed a lot in the last 20 years and the following is meant with no disrespect to the current owners who, I'm sure, have turned the place around. In 1999, the Doyle resembled the *Bates Motel* and the dreadful stories I had heard about it during the weeks prior to getting there left me with absolutely no interest in overnighting in one of its rooms.

Apparently rooms were $10 a night and there was no air conditioning. Pennsylvania in the middle of the summer is hot. Very hot. Heat rises and I imagine that the rooms on the second and third floors were likely hotter than the ambient temperature outside. I'd much rather pay $0 and sleep in my tent.

One hiker we met heading southbound who had stayed there told us the bed sheets in his room were so dirty, he laid his tent down on top of the bed and slept in his sleeping bag. And apparently the doors to most rooms wouldn't lock except the ones that had combo locks attached to them (remember the combo locks on your junior high school locker?). And then there's what happened to Baltimore Jack when he got there three or so weeks after I did.

I spoke to Jack directly about this story and other folks that were present corroborated what happened that fateful week in July of 99' at the Doyle. Now understand that Jack liked the Doyle. There was no doubt he was going to stay there as he stayed there every year he hiked through Duncannon along the Appalachian Trail. The day he showed up was a particularly hot summer day as they all are in Pennsylvania in July. He paid the $10, signed in, got his key and walked upstairs to his room. It had smelled a bit odd when he walked in the front door by the Doyle's dimly lit bar, and by the time he made it up to the floor where his room was located, it smelled quite horrifying.

Apparently the smell of a dead person is one of the unmistakable smells you could be unfortunate enough to know in this lifetime. Once you know that smell, you never forget it. I never got the backstory on how Jack knew that smell, but when the owner of the Doyle was summoned by Jack to answer the question, "What's that smell?" apparently he answered, "What smell?" to which a wide-eyed Jack said, "THAT SMELL!"

The Doyle was host to a number of long-term tenants, folks that rented rooms by the week, month and yes, even sometimes years. There was one particular tenant that the owner had not seen in a while. That particular tenant occupied the room beside Baltimore Jack's room and when they got close enough to knock on the door to see if said tenant was around, the smell went from putrid to overwhelming. The owner attempted to open the door with his key, but the door would not budge.

40

At the owner's request, Jack walked around the back of the Doyle with him and propped a 30-foot ladder against the wall, ending at the window of the misplaced tenant's room. Feeling compelled to do the owner a solid for some ungodly reason, Jack climbed the ladder and peered in through the dirty glass. Apparently the tenant was a man of larger carriage and the July heat and the estimated five days he had been deceased in a heap slouched against the door to his room had only served to add to his size. And that is why the door would not open.

Eventually the police and EMS were summoned. Hikers and the rest of the tenants were told they had to evacuate. The town's people gathered out front to try to figure out what was going on and why there were so many flashing lights and sirens. Jack realized he had left his pack up in his room and needed to get it before the place was locked down. He got permission from a cop to go get his pack and held his breath going up the stairs. I personally think that Jack wasn't able to hold his breath long enough given all the non-filtered cigarettes he smoked and the quick pace with which he charged up the stairs. At some point well before he got out of that cloud of death, he was out of oxygen. Jack took a desperate lungful of air in and proceeded to projectile vomit out the entire chicken and two liters of Hawaiian Punch that he had just consumed at the local fire department's jamboree. Jack told me that there are likely men, women and children in Duncannon, Pennsylvania, that are in therapy to this day after having witnessed what he expelled as he tumbled out the front door of the Doyle.

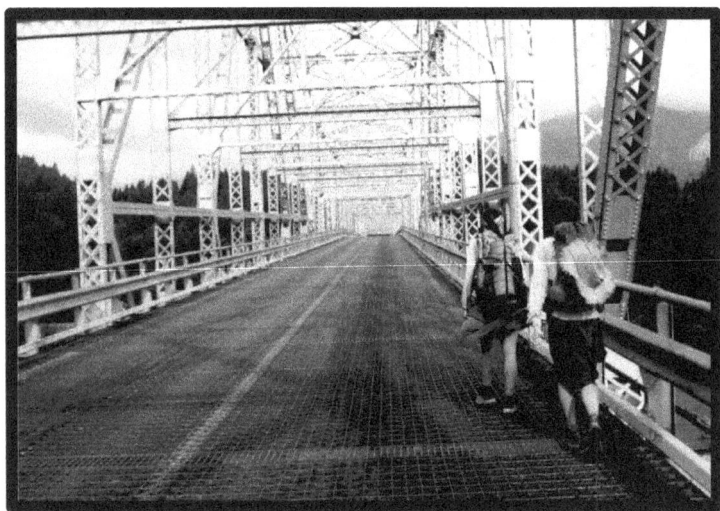

2b

TrailBro and Robert 6-Piece

As distance hikers have taken to hiking other long-distance trails more and more each year, trail celebritydom has followed suit. On the Pacific Crest Trail in 2008 the talk also centered around two hikers going far and fast and also a couple of oddballs that were out there.

Scott Williamson and Tattoo Joe were out attempting to break a speed record. They were hiking before sun up and after sun down every day in order to get from the Mexican Border to the Canadian Border in less than 82 days. They had taken to signing trail registers with their names and "sub-82." So I took to signing trail registers with my name and "sub-182." Truth be told I found what they were doing to be incredible. The PCT was difficult enough at the pace I was plodding along at and I knew it was much more difficult for Scott and Joe. And once again, I never met them on trail in 2008 because I was asleep in my tent (I figured out later) the evening they passed us in Oregon.

P.O.D. and I had started at the Mexican Border the last weekend of April that year and, as a result of not taking any days off for the first two weeks, we got ahead of the main pack fairly quickly. At our first decent town stop in Idyllwild, California, we decided to save a bit of money by forgoing a stay at one of the town's hotels to camp at Mt. San Jacinto State Park instead. That's where we ran into "The Magi." The Magi was a nervous guy with a bejeweled hat from somewhere down south who had started the trail a week before we had. There is typically no benefit in starting a Pacific Crest Trail thru-hike earlier than normal (unless it's an extreme drought year) as you end up going too early over many high mountain ranges socked in with snow as you traverse your way through the Southern California "desert" section of the trail.

The Magi had been holed up at the state park for five days waiting on Fuller Ridge's snow to melt so that he could safely cross. Fuller Ridge is a somewhat notorious stretch of PCT just north of Idyllwild that stays covered in snow much later than surrounding areas due to its north-facing exposure and abundant tree cover. P.O.D. and I hadn't thought much of slowing down for Fuller Ridge as it was an average snow year and we had heard through the trail grapevine that a number of hikers had already made it through.

"You going up there?" The Magi asked P.O.D.

"Yeah. Gotta go up there to go north on the PCT," P.O.D. said confused by the question.

"Can't go up there. Lot of snow up there. People have died up there. You'll need an ice axe and crampons, maybe snowshoes," he said.

It's human nature to project one's fears onto one's fellow humans regardless of whether or not those fears have any basis in reality. It is true that an ice axe and crampons (if you've been trained in how to use them properly) will help someone on foot traverse snowy slopes. It's also true that people have died on Fuller Ridge. People have also died on the highway near my house, but that doesn't keep me from driving my car on it.

From what we were able to surmise, our friend The Magi had never hiked on snow, which made sense, given his home deep in the Confederacy. As a result of his lack of snow experience, he was a bit freaked out.

"Fuller Ridge is gonna chew you up and spit you out faster than a pregnant woman spitting out watermelon seeds," The Magi warned P.O.D. After The Magi had wandered off to warn other hikers of their impending doom on Fuller Ridge, I asked P.O.D. if he really just said what I thought he said. She replied in the affirmative. I then asked P.O.D. what pregnant women and watermelon seeds had to do with the Pacific Crest Trail and she had no clue. Neither did I.

The next morning found P.O.D. and I hiking out at a fairly decent 8 a.m. which isn't too bad for being in town. We noticed The Magi's tent was gone as was he.

"The Magi must have gotten an early start," I offered to P.O.D.

"Maybe he went to stock up on watermelon seeds before he hit the trail," P.O.D. mentioned with a chuckle.

The Deer Springs Trail gains 2,500' over 4.5 miles as it takes hikers from Idyllwild back to the PCT at a spot called Saddle Junction. Shortly after we were back on the PCT we spotted The Magi up ahead. He was wearing full rain gear, including elbow length rain gloves, a beefy rain jacket, hiking pants, knee high gaiters, his trademark bejeweled hat and he had snowshoes and an ice axe attached to his pack. P.O.D. was wearing her hiking skirt and I was wearing shorts. We each had on sneakers and single baselayers as shirts. We had no ice axes, no crampons and no snowshoes. We were hiking on dirt and had yet to walk on any snow. The morning had started off a bit chilly, but was warming up nicely.

The Magi was hiking at a fast clip and we kept getting glimpses of him, though we never caught him. Apparently he ducked off a side trail, which we assume was on purpose. I think he psyched himself out about hiking Fuller Ridge and bailed. We never heard what happened to him.

When we got to Fuller Ridge, we found the snow to be packed down and the footpath obvious. The snow lasted for about half a mile and then it disappeared. As we hiked on I couldn't help but think that The Magi had talked himself out of something he likely would have found fairly easy because he had made it seem extremely hard in his mind.

As we made our way down the 7,000 feet of descent from Fuller Ridge to I-10 we saw "Trailbro.net" etched in the sand on the side of the trail once again. Every time I had seen Trailbro.net scrolled in the dirt by the side of the trail it made me feel like I was being forced to listen to a commercial I couldn't mute. And every time I saw Trailbro.net written in the sand on the side of the trail I spent about 10 seconds wiping over it with my foot so that my fellow hikers behind me wouldn't also be subjected to his advertising. After all, the trail is a place to get away from advertisements.... including those from Trailbro.net.

We had seen Trailbro's name in almost all of the journals that we had come across so far. He started three weeks ahead of us, which means he started way too early. In one of the journals he had mentioned starting early to get a head start on the snow. As I mentioned earlier, that's not how it works. If you start early, the snow gets a head start on you. The later you start, the less snow you have to deal with. And from what we were able to deduce from his journal entries, Trailbro also had no previous experience hiking on snowpack.

We found a frantic note he had scribbled at the trailhead for Mt. Baden-Powell. "PCT Hikers turn back! Too much snow!! You can walk Highway 2 around the mountain. If anyone finds my retainer you can contact me at Trailbro.net."

"Retainer?" I asked P.O.D. questioningly. The mental image I had created of someone named "Trailbro" did not involve dental braces or retainers. It also didn't involve someone that would walk a highway shoulder instead of the trail due to a bit of snow.

Trailbro had dated that note a week earlier. P.O.D. and I looked up from the note to see a young couple holding the hand of their toddler as they were leading him up the trail in front of us. As we headed up the nearly 3,000 foot climb from Vincent Gap near Wrightwood, California, our dirt path changed to packed snow. The trail switchbacked up and through the trees. We met a fair number of day hikers out on the trail that day, which wasn't surprising given that it was the weekend.

As the trees thinned out we spotted the famed Wally Waldron tree.... a 1,500 year old limber pine named after a noted Boy Scout leader. The Wally Waldron limber pine is reportedly the oldest tree known in the San Gabriel Mountains but 500 years younger than the limber pine known to exist in Oregon's Eagle Cap Wilderness. Wally may not be the oldest, but it's gnarled bark, twisted limbs and exposed roots nodded towards how many seasons it had seen on that windswept ridge.

We took the short but steep side trail up to Baden-Powell's summit to find a gaggle of day hikers and a group of 20 or so Boy Scouts. We weren't surprised to see the scouts given that the mountain is named after Lord Baden-Powell, the famed British army officer who started the Boy Scouts back in 1907. Hiking to Baden-Powell's summit had become a rite of passage for many local scout groups. We were surprised, though, that Trailbro had left a letter at Vincent Gap warning hikers to turn back. If 20 or so scouts and a couple with a toddler could make it to the top unscathed, surely Trailbro could have too.

A week or so later we came across another note from Trailbro regarding his retainer. It seems as though he had not yet been reunited with it. There's probably a squirrel somewhere in the San Gabriel Mountains that is wondering why it decided to use the thing to pad its nest.

We reached Kennedy Meadows at the south end of California's Sierra Mountains, and took a day off to sort our resupply box and make final preparations for an 8-9 day stretch to our next resupply point in Mammoth Lakes. As I was perusing the trail register at Kennedy Meadows, I found Trailbro's last entry. He was still a solid week ahead of us, which left me shaking my head. It was still late May and we were a bit early ourselves to be heading into the High Sierra. If we were early, then Trailbro was super early and that didn't bode well for someone who was apprehensive about hiking on snow. Kennedy Meadows is at 6,100 feet elevation. 75 trail miles later he'd be hiking/climbing over 13,200 foot Forester Pass, the PCT's highest point and a stretch of trail guaranteed to be covered in snow in May.

Late in the week we had finally made it to Forester Pass. We found the approach up to the pass itself to be relatively snowfree due to the south-facing slope. Once on top of the pass the PCT was nowhere to be seen as an ocean of snow buried the trail on it's north-facing side. We pulled out our map and were able to mostly figure out where the trail should be. There were also a few footprints leading the way in the direction of Vidette Meadow where we hoped to camp that night.

We ended up sharing our camp in Vidette Meadow that evening with a group of thru-hikers that had been right behind us all day. We were surprised to have company, but it was nice to recap the day's hike and talk trail with a couple of fellow hikers. They too were wondering about Trailbro as no one had seen or heard anything about him since Kennedy Meadows.

The following morning we reached the junction for Kearsarge Pass fairly quickly as it was only about three miles from our campsite. We found a note there from Trailbro. He had thrown in the towel and urged other hikers to do the same. His note spoke of overwhelming snow and losing the trail after Forester Pass. He decided to end his PCT thru-hike right then and there. He hiked out over Kearsarge Pass and down to Onion Valley Trailhead where he likely found a ride into the town of Independence.

I couldn't help but think once again how Trailbro started early "to get a head start" on the snow. Instead the snow got a head start on him. Seems that if you have a fear of walking on snow, you'd want to start late.... give the snow a chance to melt. Starting late would also give other hikers a chance to pack down the snow and give you the confidence to know that other hikers had made it through. I bet if Trailbro had started three weeks late instead of three weeks early, he would have made it to Canada.

~~~

Once we got north of the Sierra, the rest of our Pacific Crest Trail hike in 2008 went off without a hitch. We cruised through the rest of California, ran from mosquitoes in southern Oregon, and had fine weather through northern Oregon's Mt. Jefferson Wilderness (an area I could barely see 30 feet in any direction when I hiked through it four years prior due to fouled weather). We crossed the "Bridge of the Gods" over the Columbia River and headed into southern Washington.

The climb from the Columbia River ascends over 3,000 feet to the ridge towards which we were heading and our packs were laden with enough food to get us to Trout Lake, our next resupply point. We had been hiking with a guy named "Hearsay" and the three of us were surprised to find more than a few bottles of beer in a trailside spring late in the afternoon along with an abandoned pair of blue jeans. We each had one of the beers on the spot and took one for the road. We'd planned to have the second beer in camp later that evening. I was somewhat reluctant to carry another 12 ounces of liquid, as my pack was heavy enough, but beer won the day and I stashed the bottle into my pack.

After we crested the ridge, the thin imprint of wheel marks on the trail became more pronounced as the ground grew sandier. I chalked it up to a trail crew that had been out doing trail work. They probably had a dolly or a wheelbarrow they were using to ferry rocks or tools or both back and forth from location to location. I had been following these odd lines on the edges of the trail when I rounded a corner to find a cherubic man standing just off the side of the trail brushing his teeth. He said a garbled but cheerful HELLO with a mouth full of toothpaste.

"I'm Robert," he told us. I said hello back as did P.O.D. and Hearsay. On the ground beside Robert were two large pieces of Samsonite luggage, a large green Army duffel bag, a 10 gallon water container, a small backpack and a few other odds and ends. I looked at the wheels on the bottom of his luggage and thought about the lines on our sandy trail for the last couple miles. Not a trail crew – just Robert.

Hearsay piped in, "You been dragging that luggage up the trail?"

Robert still brushing his teeth replied, "Sure have. Started three days ago down at the river."

Without skipping a beat P.O.D. asked, "Do you want a beer? I have a cold one from the spring back there."

Robert replied, "Sure that'd be great!" P.O.D. handed Robert the beer. He twisted off the cap and without spitting out the toothpaste that filled his mouth, he started chugging the beer. He said thanks and went back to brushing his teeth.

At this point I was afraid to make eye contact with P.O.D. or Hearsay so I kept my focus on Robert. Over the next few minutes Robert would periodically remove the toothbrush from his mouth to relay a few pieces of information. He explained that he would hike a ½ mile with his backpack while pulling one piece of luggage, leave it by the side of the trail and then walk back the ½ mile to get the other piece of luggage, army duffel bag and water container. Then he would drag all that up to the first piece of luggage and start the process all over again. Every step of the trail we were doing he ended up doing three times as he walked back and forth to propel all his luggage and gear forward.

"That's a lot of luggage you've got there. Ever think about bringing less stuff?" Hearsay asked him.

"No I need all this stuff. I take it with me everywhere I go," Robert replied.

Robert went on to tell us that he lived in one of the nearby towns but was unemployed. He continued to brush his teeth as he explained that he would eat a salad every night with 15 vegetables, canned salmon and canned albacore tuna. He carried the food in his duffel bag and his clothes in the suitcases.

We bid Robert good luck, wished him well and hiked on. When I woke up that morning camped in the park at

Cascade Locks on the banks of the Columbia River, I would not have believed you if you told me I'd meet a man dragging two pieces of hard-sided travel luggage 3,000 feet up the Pacific Crest Trail. But then again, I didn't know people like "Robert 6-Piece" existed in this world. I'm glad they do. Here's to you Robert 6-Piece.

3

Ride the Lightning

My shoes squished with every step as I hiked into Tri-Corner Knob Shelter in the pouring rain. I was soaked from the waist down but dry from the waist up as I huddled under the travel umbrella I decided to bring on my Appalachian Trail thru-hike. Umbrellas have become somewhat more common and somewhat more accepted on US long trails here in 2018, but, as far as I knew, I was the only hiker using one in 1999 on the AT. I'd always get peculiar looks from other hikers back then. People would just stare. I'm not sure what they were thinking.... look at that guy in the rain using an umbrella, what a buffoon. Or.... look at that guy in the rain with an umbrella, how dare he!

There was a lady in the shelter who was giving me that look. She spent five minutes telling me why carrying an umbrella on a hike was a bad idea and how it was extra weight I didn't need and how it would get destroyed by the brush on the side of the trail and a few other things. Then she asked if she could borrow it to walk over to the privy. I laughed and handed her my umbrella.

My watch said two o'clock and I had already covered 12 and ½ miles from Icewater Springs Shelter. It was too early to call it a day and the clouds releasing all this rain were breaking up. The sun was going to pop out soon. The next shelter was almost eight miles away. Hiking there would mean doing a 20-mile day and I had never hiked that far in my life. A few of the folks I had been hiking with had done 20-milers, so I knew it was within the realm of possibility. It's just that I had never personally done one before.

The lady came back from the privy and thanked me for letting her borrow my umbrella. I grinned and told her they weren't very expensive. I encouraged her to pick one up at the next town stop. She said there was no way she would hike with an umbrella and proceeded to once more run down the list of reasons as to why hiking with an umbrella was a horrible idea. I signed the register in the shelter as she was finishing her speech, bid her and the others adieu, and hiked out.

The trail led up above 6,000' around the summits of Mt. Guyot and Old Black. Just as quickly as the storm had cleared, it moved back in. I had been hiking for only 30 minutes and pulled my umbrella out once again as the pace of the rain increased. I paused briefly, not sure if I should turn back or continue onward. It was still fairly early and I really didn't want to turn around. Plus I had no interest in being forced to hear the ridicule of the anti-umbrella lady back at Tri-Corner Knob Shelter.

I was on a ridgeline of sorts and about halfway to Cosby Knob Shelter when the rain turned into a full thunderstorm. Ugh. I had learned that when you see a flash of lightning to start counting. If you could count to five before hearing thunder that meant the lightning was one mile away. If you could count to ten then it meant that the lightning was two miles away, etc.

I was fervently counting the number of seconds between lightning and thunder as I cowered under my umbrella and quickened my pace to something between walking and a full run.

At first the storm was two miles away. Then one mile away. Then half a mile away. The rain intensified. I had visions of Ben Franklin standing there flying his kite with a metal key attached to it. He hypothesized that metal objects could draw lightning to strike them and that is what he hoped the key would prove. Turns out it worked, and, luckily for Ben, it wasn't a direct hit or else we would never have known he conducted that fateful experiment.

I decided that holding a metal umbrella over my head on a lofty, semi-exposed ridge was, in fact, not a good idea. Maybe the lady from the shelter was right? I packed the umbrella away and starting jogging (read running for my life). It's pretty silly to try to outrun lightning. Usain Bolt, the world record holding Jamaican sprinter, has been clocked running 28 mph. Lightning travels at 220,000,000 mph. Lightning wins every time.

Regardless, I jogged with my backpack on for a mile or two until the trail eventually started heading down off the ridge towards Cosby Knob Shelter. I guess running made me feel like I was at least doing something to better my precarious situation. In reality, I just got lucky. It wasn't my day to go. The storm had mostly cleared when I walked into Cosby Knob Shelter. The shelter only had space for 12 people and it was full. I slept on the dirt in front of the shelter platform that night, but was quite pleased with having hiked my first 20-mile day. I was also quite pleased that I hadn't been struck by lightning. My friend Tradja wasn't as lucky.

~~~

Each year in the United States lightning kills an average of 49 people and injures hundreds of others. The odds of being struck by lightning truly are one in a million; 1 in 1, 083,000 to be more precise. So when you hear someone say that you have a better chance of being struck by lightning than winning the lottery, they aren't just whistling Dixie.

The National Weather Service tracks lightning fatality statistics within the US. Florida has the highest rate of lightning fatalities while Texas is second. More than 70% of lightning fatalities occur during the months of June, July and August. And more than 70% of lightning victims are male. Many people assume that if it's not raining or there are not any clouds overhead then you are safe from lightning. You might be safer than if you were standing in the middle of a thunderstorm, but, as my friend Tradja learned, you are not completely safe.

Tradja and Jess were a couple that we met and hiked with a good bit on our 2006 Continental Divide Trail thru-hike. During the following summer, they were out for a short day hike near Bend, Oregon. They had been walking along the Deschutes River in a light drizzle. No thunder, no lightning, and not much of any rain. Just a light drizzle. Seemingly out of nowhere a bolt of lightning struck the tree ten feet to Tradja's left. That bolt bounced off the tree and knocked Tradja flat to the ground.

He regained consciousness fairly quickly but was unable to move his legs. Jess ran up to him, but Tradja immediately told her to get back for fear she might be struck too. She assumed the lightning crouch (more about this position later) some 30 feet or so back from Tradja. Over the next 15 minutes Tradja slowly began to regain feeling in his legs. After another 30 minutes he was able to stand up and walk.

On the walk back to their car he noticed that part of the waistband on his shorts had melted/bonded to his skin. There were some odd looking marks on his torso, too.

They drove home unsure what to do. It's not very often one finds oneself having just been struck by lightning. Jess called the Ask-A-Nurse hotline and explained what had happened to Tradja. "Do you think he needs to see a doctor?" Jess asked. "He needs to go to the emergency room right now and be examined by a physician.

Lightning can damage organs in addition to a whole host of other complications," the nurse explained to Jess.

Jess and Tradja got back in the car and drove to the hospital in Bend. They admitted Tradja and, within the next 15 minutes, most of the doctors on staff came into his examination room to see *Lichtenburg Figures* in person. Apparently that is what those weird marks on Tradja's torso were. Named after the German physicist who initially studied them, these branched red marks are caused by the rupture of capillaries beneath the skin from the electrical discharge. They are quite alarming to look at but usually disappear within a few days. He was given a clean bill of health and released from the hospital fairly quickly. On the way home he had Jess stop by a convenience store. "What do you need to get at the store?" Jess asked. "Lottery tickets," Tradja replied.

I asked Tradja if there had been any permanent damage from the lightning strike. He relayed that he experienced sporadic short-term memory loss for about a month, but that had gone away too. He also told me that his tolerance for bullshit had diminished dramatically. I can imagine going through a life or death experience would make you realize very quickly how short your time is here in the land of the living. Tradja quit his day job in the months following the lightning strike and changed the direction of his life entirely. He now works in service to the United States.... a career he had always desired but had never pursued until that fateful day hiking along Oregon's Deschutes River.

~ ~ ~

I was stuck on the section of the Continental Divide Trail between Rawlins, Wyoming, and Encampment, Wyoming, with no rain pants. It hadn't rained much at all in the last few weeks and P.O.D.'s mom thought she could sew vertical zippers down the lower legs of my rain pants so I could take them on and off without having to remove my shoes. I mailed those rain pants to her mom from Rawlins. The next day it poured cold rain relentlessly all day.

I had my trusty umbrella, but umbrella's don't do much to keep your lower body free of moisture in a wind-blown driving rain. Outside temps hovered in the low 40's all day. I was pretty miserable. I thought about the guy I met on the AT who said, "A bad day on the trail is better than a good day in the office." I wanted to slap that guy. I'd take a good day in the office any day of the week over hiking in that cold wet mess with no rain pants.

We camped behind some tall bushes off the side of the dirt road that had served as the Continental Divide Trail for most of the day's hike. My legs were freezing. We set up the tent and I immediately got in my sleeping bag. I couldn't warm up quickly enough. I had a fleece vest that I slid on and wore like a diaper. It's one of the only nights in over 1,000 nights of sleeping outside that I was too beat and too cold to eat dinner. All I wanted to do was sleep. When I told P.O.D. I was going to call it a night, she took a minute to talk some sense into me. "We've got 27 miles to hike tomorrow to meet Mary and you are going to be running on fumes if you don't get some calories tonight. I'll make something, you just stay put and get warm."

She cooked up a hot meal in our titanium pot and convinced me once again to eat as much as I could. She was right. We had 27 miles to hike the next day to meet our friend Mary at Battle Pass by 7 p.m. Mary had been taking care of our dog Gimpy over the first two months of our CDT hike. Now Gimpy was coming out to hike with us through Colorado.

The rain had stopped overnight, but the layer of clouds looked ominous to me as we were taking down our tent the next morning. Not wanting my legs to get as cold as they had the day before, I improvised a rain skirt out of our tent's plastic ground sheet. I was able to wrap it around my waist and secure it with duct tape. It hung down to my calves and worked quite well at keeping the rain that had begun again off my bare legs. I wish I had thought of the rain kilt the day before. Necessity is the mother of invention, I suppose.

Over the course of 27 miles we were hit by a series of four thunderstorms. They seemed to grow in intensity and length as the day progressed. We kept a swift pace with infrequent breaks most of the day, pushing to meet our 7 p.m. deadline and our reunion with Gimpy. With an hour to go the last of the four thunderstorms moved over us with a fury. I was initially able to count five seconds between lightning and thunder, then three, then two, then one and finally none. Pop – BOOM!!!!! The lightning flash and thunder were so close I stopped dead in my tracks with every muscle in my body tensed. I opened my eyes and was still standing. P.O.D. was up ahead, hiking as fast as I had ever seen her hike. She hadn't seen her beloved Gimpy in over two months and was bound and determined to reunite with him as soon as possible. Those two had been tied at the hip ever since she rescued him from the streets while living in Mexico a few years back. P.O.D. wasn't going to let an abysmal weather day on the trail slow her down.

As quickly as the thunderstorm bore down upon us, it moved away. By the time we arrived to a wagging Gimpy dog at Battle Pass, the rain had stopped and the skies had cleared. I asked P.O.D. if the lightning had freaked her out as much as it did me. She said she was focused on getting to the trailhead and wasn't really paying much attention. I estimate I was only ten minutes behind her and I was scared out of my mind. The next year I'd find myself in an even more dicey situation.

~~~

Summertime thunderstorms in Colorado's high country are as predictable as stripes on a zebra. Newcomers to the Centennial State will find the sky to be bright and sunny in the morning with nary a thought that things will turn at some point around lunch. Cumulus clouds usually start appearing by mid-morning and build significantly by lunchtime. Early afternoon brings a darkening to the clouds and by mid-to-late afternoon the heavens open up and the hammer of Thor is ever-present. The odd thing about the morning of July 13, 2007, is that it was already cloudy when DT and I woke up.

DT was a friend with whom I had hiked on and off during my Pacific Crest Trail thru-hike in 2004. We had kept in touch since the PCT and both had a window of time off in July. I proposed we try and hike the Colorado Trail in less than 3 weeks. Not an easy task given that we'd need to average about 26 miles a day every day with no days off. He was game and we hiked out of Waterton Canyon south of Denver on the last day of June.

The Colorado Trail meanders generally southwest from Denver to Durango. The trail covers 485 miles as it makes its way from the lower elevations near the Front Range to well above treeline in the San Juan Mountains and beyond. Most Colorado Trail thru-hikers tend to hike the trail during summer, the height of thunderstorm season. We were no different.

Oddly enough the first 12 days of our hike were rain and thunderstorm free. We had been lulled into a sense of complacency and were surprised to be hiking into camp one afternoon in a rain shower.

Given the early morning clouds we kind of figured at some point during the day we'd get hit with something. We had 23 miles of hiking left to get to Spring Creek Pass where P.O.D. would be waiting at the trailhead with our next resupply box. We'd spend most of the entire day above 11,000' and a significant amount of time above treeline. We pulled out our map and looked at various bailout options if we got caught in a thunderstorm. There were a number of lesser trails that branched off the CT descending to the north. There weren't any trails on our map that branched off heading south. The crux of the day would be the final 6.5 miles into Spring Creek Pass. There were no trails on which to bail out and we'd have to cross wide open and treeless Snow Mesa.... an infamous high elevation plateau that harbors bad weather.

I was a little quicker heading out of our first break spot that morning. As a result, DT and I played tag all day. I'd hike for an hour or so to a trail junction and take a quick snack break. DT would roll up and we'd assess the weather. So far so good. I'd take off again and the cycle would repeat.

The clouds began to get darker and darker all day. Distant rumblings of thunder had become ever present as we hiked through the La Garita Wilderness. With about ten miles to go we crossed a small stream and ascended above 12,000 feet, leaving behind the last forested campsite visible just below the trail. The weather was still holding (barely) and we discussed turning back later in the day if we needed to do so.

We passed the intersection with West Mineral Creek Trail. The wooden sign at the junction told us that San Luis Pass was 5.5 miles behind us and Spring Creek Pass was eight miles ahead. There was still plenty of blue sky intermixed with the darkening clouds. We pressed on. Eight miles to go. The trail continued to ascend across the grassy tundra dotted in the most incredible display of white, yellow and blue wildflowers. I desperately wanted to appreciate this landscape, but all I could think about was the weather.

We reached the junction with the Rough and Tumble Creeks Trail and had a discussion about our situation. This was our last bail out point before Spring Creek Pass. If we hiked forward we were committed to crossing Snow Mesa and pushing the 6.5 miles into the pass and our rendezvous with P.O.D. The skies were dark, but there was still no rain. We thought if we hustled we could likely make it to the trailhead in two hours. And the last two miles were downhill and would descend into the trees. DT and I hiked out.

We quickly passed a small pond and began undulating in and out of small ravines. Both of us already had on our rain jackets and pants in addition to putting rain covers on our packs. It seemed likely that we'd get some weather while crossing Snow Mesa and we didn't want to have to stop in the middle of a downpour to fuss with rain gear.

We hiked over a remnant snowbank and halfway across Snow Mesa it began to sleet. A few dashes of lightning off in the distance lit up the sky and the sleet changed to hail. The seconds between lightning and thunder decreased and the storm was now within a mile of our location. To our north were craggy peaks. To our south the edge of Snow Mesa dropped into the abyss. To our east was the trail behind us and to our west was the trail in front of us. We were above treeline, completely exposed and there was nowhere to go.

"Should we get into lightning safe position?" DT yelled at me across the sound of hail pelting down on my rain jacket. "I don't know. Maybe," I said, not sure what to do. "The storm is still a mile from us," I yelled, as another boom of thunder shook the ground beneath us. "If it gets any closer, we should hunker down in a ravine," I offered.

The lightning safe position or "lightning crouch" is a last resort. Getting into the lightning crouch involves first getting rid of anything metal, like hiking poles, and then crouching down like a baseball catcher on the balls of your feet. It's recommended to put your hands over your ears to minimize hearing loss and to stay crouched with your heels off the ground, but touching each other. Apparently touching your heels together increases the chances that the electricity from a ground strike would go in one foot and out the other as opposed to going in one foot and throughout the body.

Holding this position for more than 5-10 minutes is difficult. There's a school of thought that you can also sit cross-legged or kneel. And there's a school of thought that no body position will keep you safe from lightning in the outdoors outside of getting into a substantial building or metal-topped vehicle. We didn't have a substantial building or metal-topped vehicle. We didn't have anything.

Truth be told we should have been in lightning crouch way before we started asking each other if we should have been in lightning crouch. We walked as fast as we could across Snow Mesa that afternoon. DT shouted curses at the heavens and I shouted those same curses in my mind. The storm never got closer than a mile, but, given that lightning can strike as far as 75 miles away from its source, we were definitely in harm's way.

Eventually the hail turned back to sleet and the thunderstorm began to gain more distance from us. We started losing elevation and eventually descended into the trees. I took a deep breath and felt the anxiety of the last two hours slowly dissipate. I vowed never again to cross Snow Mesa on a late summer afternoon.

I spotted P.O.D.'s Subaru wagon across the highway at the trailhead. We finished the last few steps of the trail, crossed the road and staggered up to her car. She hopped out of the driver's seat, gave me a big hug and then enquired, "Did you guys get caught in that storm? It looked pretty nasty." "Yeah.... yeah we got caught in that storm," I replied.

4

Sleeping with Strangers

Tray Mountain Shelter sleeps eight and there was actually room for me. It was my fifth day on the Appalachian Trail and every shelter I had come across from Springer Mountain to Tray Mountain had been full. It became apparent that most of the "old folks" were getting up before dawn and hiking as swiftly as possible to the next shelter in order to get a spot for the next night. We'd come upon a couple of shelters where folks had arrived for lunch and then decided to call it a day and stay the night just because there was space available in the shelter to sleep. Those of us that hiked until late afternoon or early evening always found the shelters full and the folks inhabiting them to have been there for hours, if not longer. I never quite understood the obsession with sleeping under a roof when the idea of thru-hiking was to be outside.

~~~

The Appalachian Trail boasts over 250 shelters. It's the closest thing we have here in God's Country to what is commonly found along the bulk of European hiking trails. Our shelters are typically three-sided affairs which pale in comparison to the staffed huts in Switzerland. There one can sleep on a bed with sheets and be treated to a dinner with multiple courses topped off with a bottle of wine. We just aren't that civilized here in the States.

The three-sided shelters on the Appalachian Trail are spread out in such a way that you come upon one of them every 7-10 miles or so. Sometimes more often, sometimes less. There are a few things you can typically count on with the shelters along the AT: a nearby water source, a nearby outhouse (unless you are in Maine where you'll end up walking an extra quarter mile to get to the outhouse), a hard wooden floor, mice, and hikers that snore.

Eight of us packed like sardines into Tray Mountain Shelter that evening. There were lines of parachute cord running high in the shelter's ceiling. They looked like clotheslines and I was told it was proper etiquette to hang one's foodbag from the hooks under the silver reflectors dangling from the p-cord. The silver reflectors reminded me of those you'd find under each burner on a stovetop. Apparently they were slippery and big enough to keep mice from crawling down from the p-cord and reaching the foodbag attached below them.

Someone farted. Someone else laughed. "Sorry about that, too much TVP," one of the hikers blurted out. My hiking partner Titus was organizing his stuff beside me. I hesitated and then whispered, "What's TVP?"

"I don't know," he said. Another guy had overheard my question and told us it was textured vegetable protein.

"Oh ok," I said acting as if I did, in fact, have a clue what textured vegetable protein was. I grew up in the South, you see.... the closest thing we have to TVP is grits.

It takes me a while to fall asleep in the most comfortable of beds. I had a fold-out egg crate type sleeping pad and it didn't provide much cushion on the hard wooden floor of Tray Mountain Shelter. As tired as I was from the day's hike, I still couldn't get comfortable. I tossed and turned for a bit. Two hikers were already snoring, one of which would snort and gasp periodically. I think he had sleep apnea. Either that or he was practicing holding his breath until the last few seconds before blacking out at which point he'd gulp for air to keep from dying.

Within minutes of it being truly pitch black outside, I could hear the patter of rodent feet on wood. It's an unmistakable sound really. I could even hear it among the snoring and farting. This was my first night in an Appalachian Trail shelter and I didn't give much consideration to the mice as I had properly hung my foodbag.

I was almost asleep when I felt a small animal run across my face. I shot straight up with a startled harrumph and unzipped my sleeping bag as quickly as I could to do what, I don't know. The mouse had already run over my other sheltermates and retreated into a crack in the wooden wall.

I turned on my headlamp and looked around. No sign of the little bastard. I turned my headlamp off, laid back down, zipped up my bag and proceeded not to sleep at all the rest of the night. And this is what people were getting up early and hiking as quickly as possible to do night after night.

The other curious thing about those that willingly subjected themselves to this misery each evening was that 99% of them were carrying tents. They had options. They did not have to sleep in the AT shelters.... they chose to do so. This really, and I mean really, made no sense to me. They could absolutely have a mice-free and snore-free night and a much softer surface to sleep on in their tents, but decided they'd rather pack into a three-sided mousetrap with strangers that spent the better part of each night snoring and passing gas.

After my night at Tray Mountain Shelter, I avoided sleeping in shelters as much as I could for the proceeding five months as I walked from Georgia to Maine. If it was raining I'd sometimes make an exception. I did enjoy the camaraderie of all the hikers that would bunch up every evening at the shelters, however, I would typically end the day camping within a few minutes walk of a shelter. I'd go hang out, cook dinner, tell lies and then, when it was time to call it a night, I'd wish all the shelter-dwellers well and walk back to my mice-free and snore-free tent for a night of blissful sleep on soft ground. I'd pack up in the morning and walk back to the shelter to hear tales of mice or snoring or both and I'd grin. "You should try tent camping," I'd say.... "I hear it's all the rage these days."

~ ~ ~

My system of tent sleeping was flawless until the night I camped near Cherry Gap Shelter in Tennessee. Per my usual routine, I hiked into Cherry Gap Shelter around dusk and shot the breeze with the shelter-dwellers. I cooked my dinner, ate and filled up my water bottles from a nearby spring. I walked about 100 yards or so away from the shelter and found a flat spot under a hemlock. I pitched my tent, put the rainfly on, crawled in and closed my eyes.

Apparently I was so tired when I set up my tent that I forgot to do one crucial thing. Sure mice can chew through the thin nylon fabric of a tent, but they'd rather just climb through an open door. So the mouse that was going berserk and running laps around the interior of my tent at 5 a.m. had done just that as I had forgotten to zip my tent door.

I bolted upright as the panicked mouse was sprinting all over the interior of my tent. I guess he was too terrified to exit the wide open door he had entered. I unzipped my bag, fumbled for my headlamp and spotlighted him as he froze for a panicked moment in the far corner of my tent. His heart was pounding; I could see his little chest moving at 300 beats per minute. Not sure of my next move, he leaped and ran up my sleeping bag at which point I scooped and flung him right out the open door of my tent in one graceful motion. I zipped the door and sat there dumbfounded at what had just happened. I lay there until sunrise too wired to fall back to sleep. No matter how tired I was on any given night during the rest of the hike, I made absolutely sure I zipped the doors on my tent before I shut my eyes.

~ ~ ~

One thing the shelters were good for was lounging. Many of the shelters had platforms that were a foot or two off the ground, which made for a great place to sit during a midday break. It was the closest thing to sitting in an actual recliner that the AT could offer weary hikers.

One midsummer day I popped into Sam Moore Shelter way up in northern Virginia for a delicious snack of generic fig bars and off-brand potato chips. I sat on the edge of the shelter platform and leaned back on my backpack so that I was in a proper half recline similar to my favorite chair at my mom's house. No one was at Sam Moore Shelter so it seemed odd that all of a sudden there was a ruckus from inside the shelter behind me. "What the hell is that?" I asked myself as I flipped around to note the noise was coming from behind a two foot by two foot placard bolted to the wall. The placard had the "Leave No Trace" principles on it, but there was definitely a trace of something going on behind it.

To my horror I saw the partial body of a black snake swirl out from behind the placard and then three small mice peel out as fast as they could. I practically jumped out of my skin as I went from a half-reclined position to a sprint in decimals of a second. Not interested to see how this game of chase was going to end, I quickly packed my things and got out of there. I could only imagine what someone tucked into a sleeping bag against the wall of the shelter under that placard would have done. Cardiac arrest.

~ ~ ~

Then there was the day I took a break at the Manassas Gap Shelter. It was quite hot and humid as summer days in Virginia are known to be, and I was more than pleased to plop down on the floor for a midday snack and some shade. I had just torn open the wrapper of a granola bar and it was just about to hit my lips when I heard squealing and a loud scuffle underneath me. Again I almost popped out of my shoes as I jumped up and bolted to a defensive crouch on the far side of the picnic table in front of the shelter. The area between the ground and the bottom of the shelter platform was dark so it was a bit difficult to make out what was taking place. I eyeballed my backpack, which was still on the edge of the shelter platform, along with my uneaten granola bar.

The next thing that happened still gives me anxiety to this day. A rather large black snake in excess of five feet zoomed out from under the shelter followed by the largest pack rat I've ever seen. I jumped back another ten feet as they headed behind a rock off to the side of the shelter. More commotion and squealing ensued. I darted over, grabbed my pack (and granola bar) and jogged the heck out of that shelter, putting my pack on as I ran. Again I could only imagine how this would have played out if I had been sleeping in that shelter when the ruckus started. Atrial defribulation.

Apparently black snakes and mice aren't the only non-human inhabitants in Appalachian Trail shelters. Five species of skunks call the United States home. Two of those species, the striped skunk and eastern spotted skunk, frequent the Appalachian Mountains. I'm not sure which of these species bit the toe of an AT hiker sleeping in a different Virginia shelter in the middle of the night, but it has got to be one of the most unfortunate things that ever happened to this guy in his entire life.

The hiker in question instinctively kicked the skunk off the shelter platform at which point the skunk wandered over to a nearby hiker who was sleeping on a cot under a tarp. The skunk climbed onto the cot and then onto the sleeping bag of that hiker. As the hiker jumped from the cot onto the ground, simultaneously knocking the thing off of him, he sliced his foot open. The skunk continued to act aggressively towards him and another hiker in a nearby tent. This was likely the result of rabies, which causes skunks to do all sorts of odd things. The skunk met his maker that night and two of the hikers present ended up getting a full course of rabies shots as a result.

~ ~ ~

In 2010 I had a few weeks at my disposal before starting a new job and decided to use them the best way I knew how.... I went hiking. I chose to hike again from Springer Mountain (the southern terminus of the Appalachian

Trail) to Hot Springs, North Carolina, some 270 miles distant. I thought it would be neat to see how the trail differed after 11 years had passed since my original AT thru-hike.

One thing that was very different was the gear. Lots of advances in technology had occurred in the previous 11 years and, as a result, my packweight was less than half what it had been in 1999. I was now able to hike more miles with less effort. Hills that I remember as being quite nasty in 1999 barely slowed me down in 2010. I had more energy and was able to hike later into the evening of each day.

On my first day of hiking in Great Smoky Mountain National Park, it had been raining off and on all day. I was hiking under my trusty umbrella so the rain wasn't too much of a big deal, but I thought I'd stop before dark at Spence Field Shelter.

The National Park Service requires Appalachian Trail hikers to stay inside shelters within the Park. They allow hikers to camp "within eyesight of the shelter" if the shelter is full. I got to Spence Field Shelter and there were two spots left. There was a guy I called "The Smoker" who was about 30 minutes behind me. I'd been running into him off and on for the past four or five days. I didn't much care for The Smoker. It wasn't because he smoked a pack of cigarettes a day and fogged up a few of my break spots with the blue smoke from his *Camels*, it was because he was a know-it-all. See, "The Smoker" had hiked the AT the year before and he made sure everyone within earshot of his voice knew about it.

Those two empty spots in the Spence Field Shelter were for me and The Smoker. It was almost dark and still raining. I ate a bar and hiked out of Spence Field Shelter into the damp night to the horror of the shelter-dwellers. Derrick Knob Shelter was just over six miles away and that is where I'd call home that night.

I hiked through the rain up and over Thunderhead Mountain and Brier Knob. It was still raining when I strolled into Derrick Knob Shelter. I rounded the corner of the shelter's stone sidewalls and saw a smoldering fire in the attached fireplace. The shelter platform was deeply set back from its front awning, but it was obvious that this shelter that sleeps 12 had more than 12 folks in it.

I was ecstatic as I would now be able to avoid sleeping in the shelter without fear of a Park Service employee giving me a ticket. A number of the folks in the shelter saw me walk up and gave me no more than a quick glance. Then they'd turn their heads away from me so as not to make legitimate eye contact. I quickly realized why. The folks in that shelter did not want to make room for another body on the already overly crowded double-decker shelter platforms. No one said a word to me. I chuckled as I walked out to a flattish spot some 20 yards or so in front of the shelter. I pulled out my tarp and began to set it up. I occasionally glanced back towards the shelter to see shocked faces watching me set up my shelter for the night.

"I can't believe he's sleeping outside," I imagined they were saying.

"Is he crazy.... he'll never make it through the night out there. It's raining. We'll have to call search and rescue."

I don't know if they were really whispering those things, but I do know that I got a better night's sleep under my tarp than any of the 19 folks packed into that 12-person shelter. I know there were 19 because I counted them early the next morning as I hiked out just after first light.

~~~

I made good time to Clingman's Dome, which at 6,643' is the highest point on the Appalachian Trail. It's not uncommon for Clingman's Dome to be socked in with fog and this day was no different. My next goal was a low spot the trail passed through called Indian Gap. Indian Gap was a few miles shy of Newfound Gap where US Highway 441 intersects the trail and goes down into Gatlinburg, Tennessee.... a place I've successfully avoided my entire life. I had no plans to go down to Gatlinburg (after all I was out there to avoid the masses, not join them) and I knew the parking lot at Newfound Gap would be crowded with tourists. My plan was to take a nice long lunch break at Indian Gap where there'd likely be no one and then cruise right through Newfound Gap without breaking stride.

As I was taking my break at Indian Gap, a man hiked down to where I had all my wet gear drying out. He sat down right beside me and said a few things that didn't make complete sense. Then he cried for a few minutes and, just as quickly as he sat down, he got up and hiked out. I'm not sure what was going on with him and I never saw him again.

I did stop long enough to use the flush toilets at Newfound Gap. Flush toilets are a luxury to folks used to digging cat holes. It was late afternoon by now and I only had three miles to get to Icewater Spring Shelter. The climb up and out of Newfound Gap wasn't too bad and I arrived at the 12-person shelter to find only eight people there. I dilly-dallied, took my time cooking dinner, went and got the icewater from the nearby frigid spring and, by the time all that was done, four more people had shown up and claimed the last four spots in the shelter.

"Looks like I'm going to have to camp," I said to one of the shelter folks with a bit of a grin on my face. I took the Park Service's rule of camping within eyesight of a full shelter to its limit as I could barely see the roof of the shelter from the spot I chose to pitch my tent. I was able to do the exact same thing the next night at Davenport Gap Shelter, the last and final shelter within the Park.

I may rethink this strategy on the next go around after what happened to an AT thru-hiker at Spence Field Shelter in 2016. You may remember that Spence Field Shelter was the one I left right before dark so that I would not have to be bunkmates with The Smoker. Well, in 2016 an AT thru-hiker arrived to find Spence Field Shelter full so he camped in the nearby field.

At some point late that night a rather large adult black bear wandered over to his tent. He woke up to find the bear biting his leg through thin nylon tent fabric. He was able to scare off the bear and go for help at the shelter. Park service employees came out first thing the next morning to find that the bear had come back and ransacked two tents, including the tent that the attacked hiker had been sleeping in. They took the injured hiker out on a horse and he was treated at a local hospital.

Approximately 1,600 black bears live within Great Smoky Mountain National Park. That's approximately two bears for every square mile. That's a lot of bears. Couple that with the fact that Great Smoky Mountain National Park is the most visited National Park in the United States with 11 million visitors in 2016 alone. Human/bear conflicts are bound to happen.... especially with bears that have previously been fed by humans.

~~~

In addition to mice, packrats, black snakes, skunks, porcupines and various bears that visit (or take up permanent residence) at shelters along the Appalachian Trail, there's also the human factor. Not all of us are good.

By and large the 2,190 mile long Appalachian Trail is one of the safest places in the United States. That's fairly incredible given that three to four million people a year hike on some part of its length. In the last 50 years the trail has seen 11 murders. In comparison, Chicago saw 758 murders in 2016 alone.

I was hustling to get into Duncannon, Pennsylvania, on a hot June day in 1999 to catch a few of the guys I had been hiking with. I was out of water and desperately needed to quench my thirst. Four miles shy of town I came to the turnoff for the Thelma Marks Shelter, which had a nearby water source. I hesitated.

I'm not very superstitious, but I was hiking alone and I knew what had happened at Thelma Marks Shelter nine years prior to my showing up there. Two of the eleven murders that have happened on the AT happened inside Thelma Marks Shelter in September of 1990.

I walked down the steep path to the shelter. It was quiet.... eerily quiet. The shelter was one of the dingiest I had encountered along the entire trail. It had a low roof that looked as if it might fall in during the next rainstorm. The sides were built of stacked log construction back in the 1950's by none other than Earl Shaffer himself. Earl Shaffer holds the distinction of being the first documented hiker to walk from Georgia to Maine along the Appalachian Trail in a single season back in 1948. This legendary man was a local Pennsylvania resident and was responsible for building sections of the trail himself and erecting a few shelters for hikers.

Back in 1990 two southbound AT thru-hikers, Geoff Hood and Molly LaRue, had hiked the four miles from Duncannon up Cove Mountain and then down to the

Thelma Marks Shelter. Later that same day a fugitive wanted for murder in Florida also hiked those four miles to the shelter. It's unclear exactly what happened that night, but, at some point, Geoff was shot three times and Molly was stabbed eight times. Both were found in the shelter the following day.

Their killer was apprehended within the next few weeks near Harpers Ferry, West Virginia. He was hiking in Geoff's boots and carrying his backpack. He never gave a reason as to why he did what he did.

The water source for the shelter was even further down the hill than the shelter itself. I walked down and drank a liter on the spot and packed another liter out. I couldn't get out of there fast enough. It's one of the spookiest 20 minutes I've ever spent in the woods. I later learned that the shelter was dismantled and burned down a few years after I had visited it. There's a memorial to Geoff and Molly at the new shelter that was built to replace it.

~ ~ ~

In 2015, P.O.D. and I flew to New Zealand to tackle the 2,000 mile long Te Araroa trail. Te Araroa is a Maori term meaning "the long pathway." The "trail" runs from the top of New Zealand's North Island to the bottom of its South Island. Hut culture is as much a part of New Zealand as it is in Europe. Te Araroa boasts over 70 huts along the trail, most of which are found on the South Island. I remember an ecstatic hiker from Scotland telling me, "If you plan it just right, you can stay in a hut almost every single night on the South Island." His enthusiasm was lost on me as we'd been trying to avoid sleeping in huts since first encountering them for all the same reasons I was bitching about before.

The New Zealand huts were much fancier than the shelters along the Appalachian Trail. They were fully enclosed and typically contained individual bunks with mattresses, a wood burning stove, counters on which to prepare food and a mud room to change out of wet clothes. They reminded me a lot of sleeping in a bed in a house. New Zealand's weather can be atrocious, and I will say that on more than one occasion I was happy not to sleep outside during a cold slanting rain.

P.O.D. and I spent two nights in Blue Lake Hut waiting for a weather window to hike up and over Waiau Pass (pronounced Why-You) in Nelson Lakes National Park. The best thing to come out of those two days of living the hut life was meeting some great TA hikers.... hikers that we ended up hiking with and finishing the trail with. There were Matt and Bella from England, Tom from New Hampshire, Antoinne and Solenne from France and Rune from Denmark. They called Rune "the Danish Bear" because of his snoring. When asked about his legendary snoring, Rune would always say, "I don't know what they are talking about, I've never heard it myself."

Part of spending nights in huts with 15 people is dealing with snoring. I've found that the easiest way to deal with snoring bunkmates is with soft foam earplugs. Both nights in Blue Lake Hut I put in my earplugs. And even then I could hear snoring coming from the direction of the Danish Bear's bunk.

We finally got our weather window and vacated Blue Lake Hut to climb up and over Waiau Pass. The trail was steep and non-existent in places. If it weren't for the metal polls topped with high visibility bright orange plastic, we would have surely become lost. And if we'd been up there socked in by a cloud or fog, navigating would have been a total crapshoot.

We stopped at a clearing on the lee side of Waiau Pass to take a snack break and were immediately bombarded by sandflies. The sandflies that inhabit New Zealand are well-known and not in a good way. They were of the biting sandfly variety similar to New England's blackflies and they will drive you completely mad.

The odd thing about the New Zealand sandflies is that they prefer to bite exposed ankles. During trailside breaks in sandfly country, I simply draped my rain jacket over my ankles to keep them from biting and even though my head and neck were exposed, they had no interest. I'm not sure what it is about ankles that appeals to them, but I did my best to keep my ankles and lower legs covered at all times on the South Island.

As it turns out, the doors of huts aren't enough to keep sandflies from coming inside. On more than one occasion we popped into a hut to take midday refuge from the laser beam sun that shines through the hole in the ozone layer onto the southern reaches of New Zealand. And on more than one occasion we had to leave a hut rather quickly due to biting sandflies inside the hut. These were huts that people were voluntarily claiming bunk space in every night.

Even worse were the huts that had sandflies and were about ten degrees hotter than the temperature outside. I remember stopping at one of these "sauna huts" in the Richmond Range to find that a half dozen hikers had already claimed bunk spots for the night. P.O.D. and I spent ten minutes inside the hut cooking our dinner, slapping at our ankles and sweating profusely. We finished our noodles as quickly as possible and then hustled outside to set up our sandfly-free tent in the much cooler evening breezes. Every person in that hut had a tent, yet they all chose to stay in the sauna hut with the sandflies. Why, I ask you, why?

The only conclusion I've reached as to why people willingly submit themselves to this type of voluntary masochism is that sleeping under a roof with other people reminds them a bit of home. And it's what you are supposed to do when you are "tramping" around New Zealand. There's over 900 huts in all of New Zealand and, if a hut is there, why not stay in it? I can think of a few good reasons, but apparently I'm the weirdo that chooses not to be miserable.

As we made our way further down Te Araroa on the South Island, we were hiking at about the same pace as Matt, Bella, Tom, Antoine, Solenne and Rune. It was common that we'd all end up at a hut by the end of the day. Everyone would cook dinner together and talk about the day's hike and what was up ahead. Then inevitably, everyone but P.O.D. and me would grab a bunk spot in the hut. We'd go out and set up our tent somewhere nearby for a night of snore-free sleep. And then the next morning we'd hear stories of how bad Rune's snoring had been. "I don't know what they are talking about, I can't say I've ever heard it myself," Rune would plead.

Then the same thing would happen the following night. And the night after that. I didn't get it. If you knew the Danish Bear was going to keep you up all night snoring away, why would you sleep within five feet of him night after freaking night? I think that periodically he'd have a night without snoring and everyone would get this false sense of hope that his snoring had been miraculously cured. And once again the cycle would start all over the next night.

A number of us had birthdays on the trail during Te Araroa. Solenne had her birthday on the South Island on one of the nights we were all grouped up. Someone asked her what her birthday wish was. "My birthday wish is for Rune to sleep outside tonight," Solenne said with a twinkle in her eye. Rune obliged and Solenne got a snore-free night's sleep for her birthday.

The night it all came to a head was the night of Rune's and my double birthday celebration. Oddly enough, the Danish Bear and I had birthdays only one day apart and we were both turning 40. Plans and preparations were being made for a birthday celebration at a distant hut that night. Tom packed some party favors, and Matt & Bella packed steaks and a birthday cake. P.O.D. packed in a one-liter can of Russian beer for me. A bottle of wine was procured.

I can't say I've ever had steak on trail before, and I wasn't expecting much given the less than ideal cooking tools Matt had at his disposal. Somehow he managed to season and cook a delicious steak in a regular cookpot with a standard backpacking stove. The man is a culinary genius.

We stayed up a bit later than usual that birthday night and rightfully so. You only turn 40 once! I finished the large can of Russian beer and eventually called it a night. P.O.D. and I were camped out in front of the hut and, even though it was raining and we'd have a soaking wet tent in the morning, I knew it would be worth it as the hut was full of folks including the Danish Bear.

At some point in the wee hours just as the first hints of daybreak were showing themselves, I climbed out of our tent to take a leak. 33 ounces of *Baltika* beer will do that to you. In my half-awake grogginess I looked over towards the hut. On the front deck of the hut was a person sleeping on one of the mattresses from inside the hut. It was hard to make out, but it looked like Matt.

With an empty bladder I crawled back into the tent and went back to sleep. An hour or two later it was officially light out so we got up and started the preparations for the next day's hike. I walked up to the hut and a rather bleary-eyed Matt looked a bit worse for wear. P.O.D. walked up and Bella relayed what had happened during the night.

Apparently the Danish Bear was in rare form and his snoring was reverberating throughout the hut. Mice were running for cover and people were openly having conversations about smothering Rune in his sleep. Around 3 a.m., a sleepless Matt dragged the mattress from his bunk onto the deck in front of the hut. He then set up a barricade of trekking poles around his mattress to keep the hordes of Australian possums known to inhabit the area from sneaking up on him as he slept. Matt had gone to lengthy measures to set up the fence of trekking poles just right so that he was fully blocked from any and all midnight marauders.

Sometime around 5:30 a.m. Rune woke up to have his morning coffee and cigarette. He walked out the front door of the hut unaware that someone was sleeping on the deck. He walked straight into the trekking pole barricade and proceeded to knock it over and onto Matt with a loud crash amplified by the still and quiet of the early morning.

"Oh damn, I'm sorry. What are you doing out here, Matt?" Rune said, a bit startled with his bright headlamp shining right into Matt's face.

Rune was oblivious to the fact that Matt had bailed from the hut after a sleepless night due to his louder than usual snoring. "Go away. You are not talking to me today," Matt said to a perplexed Rune. The next night everyone slept in a hut again with Rune. Everyone but P.O.D. and me.

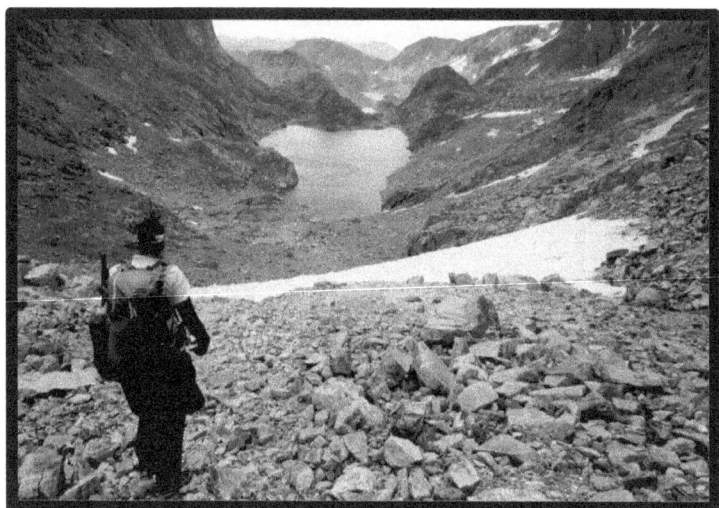

5

Exit Crack

The opening scene to the 1993 action adventure film *Cliffhanger* shows one Gabe Walker, played by none other than Sly Stallone, desperately trying to save stranded climber Sarah (the girlfriend of one his buddies), played by Michelle Joyner. Gabe is frantically attempting to get Sarah clipped onto a rescue cable when a clip on her climbing harness breaks and she starts to free-fall. Gabe reaches down and is able to grab her forearm with one hand as she dangles thousands of feet above a rocky abyss.

"Sarah I got ya, just reach up," Gabe implores as he is dangling upside down trying to not lose hold of her. Sarah's grasp starts to give way as her hand slides down Gabe's forearm. "Don't let me die!" she screams at Gabe. The camera zooms in and we see her hand slip out of her climbing glove. Sarah plunges (in slow motion of course) to a terrifying death. Gabe is left hanging upside down in his climbing harness in tears. I thought of this scene almost every day for a month after P.O.D. and I got back from the Wind River High Route.

~ ~ ~

Wyoming's Wind River Range is a gem. It covers over 2.25 million acres of land and contains 40 named peaks over 13,000' in elevation including the highest mountain in Wyoming, Gannett Peak. Seven of the largest remaining glaciers in the Rocky Mountains are found in the Winds as are over 1,300 named lakes. An incredible section of the Continental Divide Trail is located in the Wind River Range as is the southernmost population of grizzly bears in the lower 48. It sees a fraction of the crowds that California's High Sierra sees, which made it the perfect place for a quick escape in August of 2015.

We had hiked through the Winds in 2006 on our southbound thru-hike of the Continental Divide Trail from Canada to Mexico. The Winds had been a true highlight of our CDT hike and a place we had vowed to return to one day. Well, that day had come and we were headed back for six days of no work, no cell phones, no distractions and a chance to do one of the things we love to do together: go for a hike!

This time would be different, however, as we wanted to explore some of the other trails in the Winds while figuring out a way to do that with only one car. That left two options: A) we could do a loop hike starting and finishing at the same trailhead, or B) we could hire someone to shuttle our car from the trailhead where we began to the trailhead where we hoped to finish. The risk with Option B is that something could happen during the hike to keep us from finishing at the distant trailhead where our car would be waiting.

We had heard rumblings of a "Wind River High Route" that would take you off the CDT onto some more obscure but also more scenic trails. We didn't want to take rock-climbing gear or get into anything too technical. We just wanted to go backpacking but also explore some of the Wind's more off-the-beaten paths and some of the places we had purposely avoided back in 2006.

On our thru-hike in 2006, we took the most benign route through the Winds that we could find. There were lots of alternates listed on our Jon Ley CDT maps: Cirque of the Towers, Knapsack Col, Jackass Pass, Titcomb Basin, etc. Most of our fellow hikers explored all of these places. We avoided these places partly because we didn't want to carry the extra couple of days of food that would have been required, and partly because we didn't think our hiking capabilities were up to the demands some of these alternate routes commanded. In 2006 we were content with simply hiking the Continental Divide Trail as it was plenty tough enough on its own.

We'd be hiking all of these alternate routes and much more on our traverse of the Wind River High Route. It's worth mentioning that there are multiple Wind River High Routes out there, but the one we chose started at Green River Lakes and traveled 80 miles to the trailhead down at Big Sandy. We had been quoted over $350 to have our car shuttled from Green River Lakes to Big

Sandy. We decided that was too much money to spend on a six-day hike.

An examination of our maps showed another option. We could drive to the town of Pinedale on the west side of the Winds and then up to the trailhead at Elkhart Park. We'd hire someone in Pinedale to shuttle our car from that trailhead over to the Big Sandy Trailhead, which is also on the Pinedale side. $75 done and done.

The beauty of this option is that we'd still get in about 80 miles of hiking although we'd take a different set of trails on our first day to link into the good stuff in the High Country.

We made arrangements with the shuttle service in Pinedale, drove up to the trailhead, stashed the key and started hiking with our fingers crossed that both we and our car would magically appear at the Big Sandy trailhead six days later. I stashed a few beers in the trunk for what I hoped would be a celebratory finish.

We took a series of well-trodden trails by a scattering of lakes to get to the Continental Divide Trail. Once on the CDT we hiked north towards Cube Rock Pass and Peak Lake where we would divert off the CDT to go up and over the infamous Knapsack Col. Knapsack Col sits at 12,260' and is simply a notch between two mountains. This notch separates Peak Lake from Titcomb Basin, our next destination. We had been afraid of Knapsack Col in 2006 having heard many a tale about how steep it was, how difficult it was and how we'd never make it without carrying days upon days of extra food and technical gear. This time around we hiked the nearly 2,000 feet of uphill to get there without hesitation!

Knapsack Col is incredible. The hike up was slow going and the randomly spaced cairns definitely helped keep us on track. The scene looking east from the Col was otherworldly and one of the most astonishing alpine landscapes I've ever set foot in. Jagged 13,000' peaks rose up in front of us. Granite rock blanketed by fat white clouds covered the sky. This was the land of rock and ice. I had been worried that we'd find the descent off the east side of Knapsack Col covered in snow and ice from Twins Glacier. The glacier had receded to a sprawling field of dirty looking snow well above the main gulley from which we'd descended down to Titcomb Basin. Nothing to worry about at all.

The hike around the east side of Titcomb Lakes was as scenic as everyone had said it was. Some folks come into the Winds just to backpack to Titcomb Basin and I could see why. Our route eventually ducked off the main Titcomb trail and headed up Indian Basin and Indian Pass.

Wildflowers lined the path ahead. The reds of the scarlet paintbrush were vibrant as were the purples, yellows and whites of an untold number of wildflowers. Summertime in the Winds is a remarkable thing to behold.

We reached Indian Pass early on the morning of Day 3. Two guys and a Rottweiler were up there taking a break when I arrived just ahead of P.O.D. We talked trail and I learned that they had just come across the Alpine Lakes Basin and Knife Point Glacier where we were headed. Their dog's paw pads were in rough shape. They had taken a couple of days to get through Alpine Lakes Basin so I didn't mention that we planned to get through by mid-afternoon that same day. I try to avoid the "you're never going to make it" conversations when possible.

As P.O.D. and I hiked onto melting Knife Point Glacier, the sky had begun to darken and blend in with the dirty snow and ice that comprised the glacier's diminishing surface. The glacier sloped downward, but the angle wasn't too steep so traversing across safely was doable. My fears about the Wind River High Route were starting to subside. Knapsack Col had been a bit easier than I had thought it would be, as had been traversing this glacier.

We passed by a number of gargantuan boulders that were taller than we were as we stepped off the edge of the glacier and back onto bare rock. During the few hours we had spent on Knife Point Glacier, we heard the loud crash of rockfall above the glacier and the constant sound of flowing water beneath us. I couldn't help but think that the glacier was thawing under our feet and that it wouldn't be around for many more years. I was glad we got to experience what was left of it before it is gone.

By the time we crested Alpine Lakes Pass, the sky was dark and rain looked imminent. The research we had done on our route through the Alpine Lakes Basin showed that this would be the toughest part of the entire hike, culminating in our exit of the basin by going up a rock chute that would require a few Class 4 moves. The map labeled this the "exit crack."

The class system for hiking and climbing is as follows: Class 1 is just hiking. Class 2 involves simple scrambling with the possible occasional use of hands. Class 3 is scrambling with the use of hands, and a rope might be needed, and there might be some exposure to heights. Class 4 is simple climbing but often with exposure. A rope is often used and a fall could be fatal. And Class 5 is legit rock climbing involving a rope, belaying and protection.

We had reached out to some friends of P.O.D.'s that had hiked the same version of the Wind River High Route that we were doing. Both of them were shorter than we were and said the "exit crack" had been no problem. Plus P.O.D. had just finished the Sierra High Route, which involved days of scrambling on talus. Her skill level had increased by leaps and bounds and she had no qualms about our getting up and out of the exit crack.

As we descended towards the northwest corner of the uppermost lake in the basin, it started to rain lightly. We stopped to put on our rain gear and resumed hiking. I thought to myself that not only was this going to be our toughest day on the High Route, but we'd be doing it in the rain. Rain makes everything slippery so we had to be diligent and methodical about every step.

The notes we had about the start of this section said to hike along but stay above the west shore of the uppermost lake. "The cliffs along the shore appear impassable, but go. Not visible from a distance is a short Class 3 ramp system (climb up and down) near the lakeshore that allows passage to a flatter section near the lake's outlet."

We read the notes over and over as we were approaching the cliffs and I was frankly horrified at what I was seeing. The cliff band was steep and it dropped straight into the lake. The ramps being referred to were one to three foot wide strips of tundra between rocks that appeared to drop off at the edge of various cliffs into the abyss. P.O.D. had mentioned having to descend via "ramp" systems on the Sierra High Route and didn't seem too perplexed by the puzzle in front of us.

At my urging we descended all the way to the lake's edge. Surely there was a way to walk the shoreline down to the other end of the lake. We got to the shore only to find an impassable section of cliffs dropping straight into the water. Unless we were up for a swim, there was no getting around the mass of rocks rising up from the lake.

We started slowly back up the talus, looking for the ramp system as we ascended. We spied a flatter piece of ground a hundred or so feet above us. It looked like we'd have to ascend 200 feet to the right and then scramble back down 100 feet to get there. This jived with what our research on this route had told us. P.O.D. decided that she didn't want to go up 200 feet just to come back down 100 feet. And that meant doing some free climbing, unroped, to get to the plateau where we assumed our magic ramp would be. "You're crazy. Why would you climb up there? If you fall you're going to get hurt," I said with a grimace. "I've got this. I'll meet you up there," P.O.D. said with enough confidence that I didn't second-guess her.

I scrambled up the 200 feet, went around a small cliff band and then scrambled down the 100 feet to the plateau that we had been eyeing. I could barely look at P.O.D. because I was freaked out that she was free climbing. It took her another 10 minutes to get to where I was waiting on her. "I probably shouldn't have done that," she said to me, somewhat exasperated. The knot in my stomach slowly unwound as she sat down beside me.

The rain began again in earnest and we talked about not taking any more chances for the rest of the day. I had a SPOT device, (essentially a 911 button that uses satellites to summon help) but a rescue would take a long time out here in the middle of nowhere. We didn't want to get ourselves into a situation where we needed to use that SPOT device.

We had a quick snack and then walked out on the plateau, thinking it was the ramp system that would lead us safely through the cliffs and out to the lake's outlet. The plateau ended abruptly in a 50-foot sheer drop onto more rocks. This obviously wasn't the correct ramp. When in doubt, go uphill.

So we ascended the talus looking for green ramps that traversed off to our left. We passed almost a dozen that all looked precarious and undoable and then we stopped as it seemed as though we had gone up too high.

I turned on my GPS unit to get our exact position. The GPS showed that we were now 300 feet higher than the red line on our map. The red line represented our route through the cliff band. It started raining harder and my anxiety went up another couple of notches. "I've got to take a shit. I'll make it quick," I said to P.O.D. as I found a few boulders to hide behind. After my "stress shit" was over, I immediately felt better but went back to anxiety rather quickly. We had to retrace our steps ever so slowly back down the mountain to find the ramp that continued to elude us. We got to the first one rather quickly and it looked steep, narrow and terrifying.

"We've got to walk out to the end of each of these ramps to see if they *go*," P.O.D. said resolutely.

"They all look like a nightmare," I said slightly panicked. "How can any of them go?" I asked.

"One of them has to go. Our friends made it through. There has to be a way," P.O.D. said.

So we came to each of the green ramps and walked them out as far as we could go. They all dead-ended at the edge of a sheer drop that would spell disaster.

We were walking out the fifth or sixth one to find that it initially looked terrifying, but we couldn't see the totality of it. We crested a small rise that obscured our line of vision. This was *the ramp*. This ramp did in fact "go!" I looked at my watch. We had spent two hours hiking up and down this area trying to find this specific ramp. This would have taken ten minutes at most if we had actually known where it was. Two hours.... in the rain.

No time to cry over spilt milk. You don't know what you don't know as the saying goes. We found the ramp and now had to beat feet to get to the lower lake and our rendezvous with the "exit crack."

We hiked past the lake's outlet and then skirted the west edge of a middle lake. The route forward was on a jumble of talus but wasn't too difficult to navigate. From the end of the middle lake we traversed over to the north and east side of the lower lake. Our map showed the exit crack at the far east end of the lower lake and then we'd descend back into the trees, which I was more than ready for as the rain dripped off my hat brim.

About halfway along the north shore of the lower lake we came upon the perfect overhang under which to take a break. We had to crouch to get underneath a big rock slab that pitched out like an awning. We hadn't stopped more than ten minutes since leaving Indian Pass early that morning. It was now mid-afternoon and we were both feeling a bit beat.

Apparently we weren't the only ones under that rock overhang. An angry chipmunk popped out from under a rock and raised all manner of hell for invading his space. It made sense that an animal would call this protected cubbyhole home. "We'll only be a few minutes," I said as he dashed back under a jumble of smaller rocks. He proceeded to squeak at us for the entire 15 minutes we sat there out of the rain. We both stuffed our faces as we knew we'd need some calories for the exit crack.

I had my GPS on as we hiked out of our little cave. I wanted to make sure we navigated to the exact spot where the exit crack was located. I glanced at the notes we had about the exit crack:

> *"It is plain sailing along the shore until you are almost to the outlet where a 50-100 foot section of cliffs ruins the party. We climbed a Class 3/4 crack system above a stand of white pines (handing packs up in a few places) for approximately 75 feet to gain flatter ground above the cliffs. We then descended gentle ramps to the outlet. Views from outlet of this lake are stupendous. It would make an excellent lunch spot or campsite."*

We hiked until we reached the section of small cliffs that would be the final hurdle of the day. A steady rain was falling and I shook my head as I thought about how the lake's outlet "would make an excellent lunch spot or campsite." Not today it wouldn't.

We used our GPS and map to navigate to what we thought was the exact spot to go up the crack in the cliffs. The notes had mentioned "a stand of white pines." The spot where we stood had a few dwarfed spruce trees. Hmm. I thought that maybe the notes had the incorrect tree species (not many people know or care about the differences between pines, spruces, firs, junipers, etc. I happen to know the minutiae of such things because I work as a Forester in my other life). In the end, I decided there was a small mistake in the notes with the listed tree species and that we were, in fact, at the right crack.

From our vantage point at the base of the cliffs, it appeared there was a series of three or four narrow ledges we would have to climb up and over in order to get to a point where the rocks ended and a slightly sloped plateau of tundra began. If we could get to that tundra, we'd be good to go. I started up first. The rocks were slick from rain, but the footholds were pretty decent. I made it up to the first ledge and told P.O.D. to hand up her pack. I laid on my stomach and reached down as she hoisted her pack above her head to hand it to me. I grabbed the pack and then she climbed up to the ledge on which I was perched.

Ledge two wasn't that bad either. I took my time placing my feet on little rocky nubs protruding from the rock face as I checked and rechecked the handholds I was using for firmness. I made my way almost to the top and then swung my leg up and onto the second ledge and hoisted myself up. I reached down and grabbed P.O.D.'s pack once again and brought it up to where I was sitting. P.O.D. climbed up without too much difficulty and we prepared for ledge three.

Ledge three was higher above us and there weren't as many obvious spots to place our hands and feet. There was a bit of a crack in the rock running vertically up the left side towards the ledge above. I was able to climb up to a spot where I could jam my fist into the crack and then use my jammed fist to pull myself up to the top of the ledge. One last move and exertion of energy got me up and over the top onto a narrow sitting area. I was able to lie on my stomach again and grab P.O.D.'s pack as she threw it up to me. There was barely any room on the ledge to place the pack. I looked down at P.O.D. and immediately the knot in my stomach started to grow.

P.O.D.'s first few tries at stepping up onto the tiny rocky nub that I had used as my first step resulted in her sliding back down the rock face. The rocks were slick from the rain, which had now increased in pace. Finally she got enough purchase to push up and then place her free foot on the next nub. She pushed up again and was now at the spot where I had jammed my hand in the crack to pull myself up. She hesitated.

From my perch on the narrow ledge I could see down past her to both the ledges below and the steeply sloping talus rock by the spruce trees where we started up. A fall here would be really, really bad. Alarm bells started sounding in my brain. Red flags were going off in my mind. I immediately felt the need to puke. We were in a bad place. We were in a place we shouldn't be. We were now doing a Class 4/5 climb, unroped, on wet rock, in the rain. My SPOT device was in the front pocket on my backpack's shoulder strap. I squeezed it just to make sure it was still in there.

I did my best to remain calm. "Try to get your hand in this crack and then you can pull yourself up and put your foot on that point," I said as I reached over the ledge and pointed to the small rocky protrusion where I had put my foot. P.O.D. reached up and got her hand wedged into the crack and then pulled herself up. When she went to place her foot on the rock, it slipped. She tried a few more times and her foot kept slipping. I instinctively reached down and grabbed the forearm below her free hand at which point her other foot slipped.

I was now holding P.O.D. as both her feet were dangling. I've never had more adrenaline shoot through my body during a day of hiking than at that very moment. "You're good. Just put your left foot back on the rock it was on," I said calmly. She did. "Now put your right foot on that little rock sticking out." She moved her right foot up until she was almost on top of it. "That's it. Right there," I said. She was now able to relax just a bit. I was ready to puke again. "On three I'm going to pull you and you are going to push up with your right leg. You'll be able to get your butt onto the ledge," I tried with confidence to say. "1, 2, 3," I said, as P.O.D. pushed up at the same time I pulled her up. She twisted around and got her butt on the ledge and we paused for a moment sitting there in the pouring rain.

We still had one more ledge to get up and over, but this one was short and straightforward. We both made it up and onto the tundra. We then made our way to a spot where the tundra started gently descending to the lake's outlet. "Can we stop for a minute?" I said weakly. I sat down and put my head in my hands. I felt nauseous. "That's the most incredibly stupid thing we've ever done," I said, reliving the moment of her feet dangling while I was holding her arms. "If you had fallen you would have broken something or worse," I said, staring off into space. I felt numb. I felt sick.

~~~

The rest of the hike was mostly uneventful. I had a hard time not playing the exit crack day over and over in my head though. Every night for the rest of the trip I thought about it as I was falling asleep. It makes me sick to my stomach to this day to go through what happened on those ledges.

Once back home we had a debriefing of sorts and went back over our notes and talked to P.O.D.'s friends again. We determined that we took the wrong crack up and out of those cliffs. After P.O.D.'s friends described their ascent of the exit crack in detail, it was obvious that our ascent was on a different piece of rock.

There was also an option to hike around the other side of the lower lake, which would have added two miles to the hike but avoided the cliff band altogether. It's easy to analyze all these scenarios when sitting in the friendly confines of one's home. It's a different ballgame when you are actually there, tired, soaked from a cold rain, just wanting to get it over with.

In retrospect, we should have taken the long way around the lake and avoided the exit crack on that rainy day. We didn't. We were dumb. But we were lucky. And we'll never do something that stupid again.

6

18 Holes on the Pacific Crest Trail

"His name is Flounder," the scruffy kid from Pennsylvania announced as Flounder walked up to the shelter alongside the Appalachian Trail.

In unison everyone at the shelter said, "Hi Flounder!"

Flounder looked at all of us and then at his friend from PA and said, "My damn name isn't Flounder," to which we all had a mighty laugh.

Flounder had been hiking with a group of three other guys in their early 20's. They were all from the same town in Pennsylvania and all knew each other quite well. The first three guys in the group had earned their trail names fairly quickly. Since Steve was still going by Steve, they got together one night and decided that they would start telling everyone that Steve's trail name was Flounder. And it stuck. Especially after Flounder started getting pissed off that people were calling him Flounder.

Eventually he warmed up to the name and went with it. I've known a lot of hikers since meeting Flounder on the

AT in 1999 that have broken protocol and given themselves their own trail names just so they wouldn't end up with a garbage trail name that they hated.... like Flounder.

~~~

There's lots of shenanigans that take place on long trails. It makes sense as people have a lot of time to think while out walking 2,000+ miles. And even though friends and family back home believe that you are on a great action-packed adventure, the truth is that the days can be long and uneventful and the boredom unrelenting. People do what they have to do to keep the tedium at bay.

By the time P.O.D. and I reached New Mexico we were almost four months into our southbound thru-hike of the Continental Divide Trail in 2006. The terrain had mellowed out a bit and we found ourselves walking a lot of dirt roads in northern New Mexico. We had been hiking with our buddy Skittles and one cold morning I had walked a bit ahead of P.O.D. and him. I was wearing a black balaclava that covered most of my face to stay warm in New Mexico's chilly autumn air. The rest of the drab clothes I had on kind of blended in with the forest and I guess I looked like some type of timber ninja. I silently crept off the side of the trail and squatted down beside a small pine. I waited there quiet as a mouse until P.O.D. and Skittles walked by at which point I jumped out from my hiding place and shouted "BIDAH!!!" as loud as I could. Both of them jumped a few steps backwards and then laughed after realizing they weren't being attacked by a group of Santa Fe black belts. I filmed the whole thing as I was shooting video for *The Walkumentary*.

I don't know why I jumped out and scared them. I was bored. I really did think I looked like a ninja. And I thought it would make for good film.

And I don't know why I yelled the word "BIDAH" as this really isn't a word. It was a man's name. Bidah was the guy who was running the motel in Mojave, California, back in 2004 when I hiked the Pacific Crest Trail for the first time. My friend Jupiter stayed at that motel the same few nights I did and, when she first got to her room, she noticed the sheets on her bed looked a little disheveled. She peeled back the comforter to find a brown circular stain of unknown origin on the otherwise white sheets. She called the front desk to make the manager aware of the situation.

"I just checked into Room 205 and the sheets on my bed are soiled," an annoyed Jupiter said to the man on the phone.

There was a longer than usual pause. "Maybe it was you that soiled the sheets," the manager replied.

Jupiter was not having any of this and let the guy know in no uncertain terms that he could fix the situation or refund her money. He fixed the situation and we later learned his name was Bidah. I hiked on and off with Jupiter over the next three months on the PCT and I would randomly say to her, "Maybe it was you that soiled the sheets" to which we would both laugh (me more than her).

Anyway, I was so encouraged by both P.O.D. and Skittle's reaction to my yelling "BIDAH!" at them that I spent the next three weeks plotting and scheming everyday when I could jump out of the bushes again. I did it enough that I devoted an entire segment of *The Walkumentary* to this ridiculousness.

Apparently other hikers saw the film and started doing the same thing to their friends. Two years later P.O.D. and I hiked the Pacific Crest Trail together and I was shocked to meet two guys that were calling themselves the "Bidah Brothers." They had seen the film and were constantly hiding in bushes and jumping out to scare their friends. I had inadvertently created a few monsters when the reality was that I was just trying to unbore myself.

~~~

Before Jupiter's incident at the motel in Mojave, I had been hiking behind a group of three reprobates, Sprite, Skywalker and Goat, who had taken to playing pranks on each other to pass the time. In addition to hiding off the side of the trail and jumping out to scare the bejeezus out of each other, Sprite had taken to hiding Skywalker's shoes.

Shoes are the wheels that keep a long-distance hiker rolling. A hiker without shoes is like a pitcher without a baseball. I've known a few hikers that have awoken in the middle of the night to find that a curious deer in need of a salt fix had stuck its muzzle under the vestibule of their tent to pull their shoes out to munch on them. Those hikers gave chase and got their shoes back, opting to keep their shoes well inside their tents at night from there on out. Again, without your shoes, you're no longer a hiker.... you're just an unemployed barefoot bum in the woods.

The first time it happened to Skywalker, he woke up to find that Sprite and Goat had packed up and hiked out early. He had kept his shoes on the ground beside him and he immediately knew that it was no coincidence that Sprite and Goat were gone and his shoes were gone, too. Not knowing what else to do, he packed up and gingerly hiked out barefoot.

It's true that humans can walk through forests barefoot and get to a point where they can walk just as fast barefoot as they would with shoes on. This takes time though. You've got to build calluses and get the skin on the bottom of your feet to toughen up. If you've been walking around in shoes all your life, immediately going barefoot on trail is a shock to the system. Every pebble, rock, root and imperfection feels like an assault on the sensitive skin of feet that haven't seen bare ground since childhood. Such was the half mile that Skywalker plodded until he found his shoes sitting in the middle of the trail with a note from Sprite.

"Thought you might need these. Love, Sprite," the note read.

Skywalker put on his shoes and hiked fast to catch up with Goat and Sprite. What he didn't realize is that Goat and Sprite were also hiking fast, knowing Skywalker would be coming after them. He didn't catch them until late in the day and by then his anger had subsided a bit. After hearing about all of this, I made sure to either keep my shoes in my tent at night or use them as a pillow if I was cowboy camping. I figured I'd wake up pretty fast if someone pulled my shoe pillow from under my head.

~~~

On the Continental Divide Trail in 2006 we were hit with three snowstorms in Colorado in September. It's not unheard of to have September snowstorms in Colorado's high country, but having three in a row is just plain bad luck. The first two dumped less than a foot of snow and melted pretty quickly. The last one dumped two feet of fluffy white stuff on the divide.

Two feet of snow came up to my knees. Trying to hike through knee deep snow is slow going, to say the least. We all took turns "breaking trail" and punching through the snow. Our friend Speedo had been hiking with a gal named Lovebarge and he rather enjoyed breaking trail because he's a sadistic man who gets bored easily and this was something new. Lovebarge offered a couple of times to lead the way to which he would reply, "I am half Finnish. The Finns have a proud tradition of breaking trail in the snow. I must break trail."

Hours upon hours went by and Lovebarge had not offered to break trail any longer as she was pretty beat. Speedo noticed that Lovebarge wasn't looking around.... she was just plodding along in the exact path that he was creating as he broke trail in front of her. She had her head down and was in forced march mode. He grinned as he started subtly veering from the path and he noticed that she didn't even look up. She just continued following the path he created through the snow. At this point, he started walking up embankments on the side of the trail and zig-zagging all over the place. Lovebarge continued to hike in silence with her head down. Speedo was snickering to himself as he went straight up a steep hillside well off trail. Lovebarge finally looked up and Speedo burst out laughing.

"What the hell, dude, you've been hiking all over the place," Lovebarge said accusingly, having been jostled out of a mindless stupor.

"I know, you weren't paying attention and were following me wherever I went," he said with a laugh.

"Move over. I'll lead the way," Lovebarge said as she walked by a doubled over Speedo.

~ ~ ~

Getting to Kennedy Meadows on the Pacific Crest Trail is a big deal. It marks the end of the desert section, which begins the moment you hit the trail at the Mexican Border. 650 miles is a milestone, which seems odd now that I write it, given that once you get to Kennedy Meadows you still have another 2,000 trail miles to Canada. Regardless, we were in the mood to celebrate.

I had been hiking off and on with a rather large contingent of hikers collectively known as "The Unit." We had hiked close to 25 miles to get to Kennedy Meadows and were beat and a bit dehydrated. Beers were procured and I had a rather large helping as did everyone on the porch that night.

We stayed up late telling lies and hashing over the previous six weeks on the PCT. Somebody was playing music and the hours passed by all too quickly. After having a few more beers than I should have, I wandered over to the abandoned amphitheater on-site and lay down on the ground between two rows of bench seats. It was sometime around two in the morning. Sleep came rapidly.

Three or so hours later I cracked open my eyes at 5:15 a.m. My brain felt like someone had taken a jackhammer to its frontal lobe. To say I was hungover is being nice. I felt like the innards of a building that had just been brought down with a two-ton wrecking ball. Hiking 25 miles in the southern California summer heat and then drinking a small vanload of Coronas is not the best way to find optimal health.

I lay there for another three hours in too much discomfort to sleep or stand up. Sometime after 8 a.m. I bought a soda from the vending machine and drank it in small sips; my stomach wouldn't allow anything more. I walked back to the amphitheater with a splitting headache and grabbed my stuff. I needed a shady spot to hide from the day.

Just outside the perimeter of buildings at Kennedy Meadows, I found a nice Douglas-fir tree with soft flat ground underneath. I laid out my sleeping pad and pulled my hat over my eyes. I periodically got up every few hours to move my sleeping pad as the sun continued to arc south and then west, spotlighting me in the face.

By late afternoon my headache had subsided and I was hungry. I gathered my belongings and walked back to the porch with my shades on as the sun was still bright and my hangover had not completely gone away. I slowly ate a burger and slowly came back to life. I vowed to never hike 25 hot miles again, followed by drinking large quantities of low rent beer.

I spent the rest of the day rehydrating and making preparations for the hike out of Kennedy Meadows and into the High Sierra. I went to sleep that night in the amphitheater again, but couldn't find my hiking poles. I had them earlier that day, I thought, but couldn't find them. I figured I'd find them the next morning and went to sleep.

I spent the better part of two hours searching for my hiking poles the following morning. I had moved around a lot during hangover day and had moved all my stuff around with me. I searched the amphitheater, the area around the Douglas-fir tree, the porch and other various buildings at Kennedy Meadows. Nothing.

I took to asking hikers if they had seen a pair of blue Leki hiking poles. No one had. Then I asked Ukelele Nate who told me his brother Salami had a pair of hiking poles on a picnic table that he was getting ready to hacksaw. "WHAT!?" I yelled, as I ran back over to the picnic table beside Kennedy Meadow's big wraparound porch.

The picnic table where Salami was sitting at looked like an operating table. He was sitting there with a hacksaw (yes, a hacksaw!) and some tools he had borrowed from the folks at the store. He also had my blue Leki hiking poles, which he had taken apart and had meticulously laid out beside the hacksaw. He looked like a surgeon preparing to operate.

"Dude, what the hell are you doing? Those are my hiking poles," I said both bewildered and angry.

What hiker carries a hacksaw in their backpack? I've known hikers that carry odd things: a teddy bear, a Frisbee, a full-sized pillow, blue jeans, etc. But a hacksaw??? Never a hacksaw.

"These aren't your hiking poles. I found them under a tree over there," Salami motioned, pointing in the exact direction of the big Douglas-fir where I had spent the bulk of the previous day.

"Um, yeah, those are my hiking poles. I was sleeping under that tree yesterday and left them there," I said reaching across the table to grab them.

At this point Salami realized I wasn't bullshitting him. "Oh, sorry dude, I didn't think they were anybody's," he said somewhat sheepishly.

"Why the hell do you have a hacksaw?" I asked, dumbfounded.

"Oh, you never know when you might need to cut through a lock or get through a gate," he replied as if every hiker carried a hacksaw while on trail.

I shook my head as I walked away. My late night Corona free for all had almost cost me my hiking poles, which would have been a disaster, as the tent I was carrying required two trekking poles to create its frame and could not be set up otherwise. The joke was almost on me. Again I vowed to never hike 25 hot miles, followed by a late-night bender.

~ ~ ~

Having your hiking poles hacksawed by a fellow hiker is unfortunate. But this was child's play compared to what happened to my old hiker friend, Baltimore Jack (*requiescat in pace*).

Jack kept unfortunate company from time to time. He was out on the Appalachian Trail most every year hiking either the entire thing or a big chunk of it. He routinely made a point to take a few days off in Damascus, Virginia, during the Trail Days event in May. Trail Days is the big annual gathering of AT Hikers. Hikers from years past and many of those hiking during the current year make a point to go to Damascus to celebrate. And why not.... walking over 2,000 miles from Georgia to Maine is an incredible thing to do!

I'm not sure what disgraceful thing Jack did to his associates to warrant what they did in return, but apparently they knew where Jack's tent was set up. At some point earlier that day they were driving to Damascus and spotted some fresh road kill on the side of the highway. It's unclear exactly which *Genus* the animal belonged to as it was a bit mangled, but it was just about the right size to fit easily into Jack's backpack.

As the plan was being hatched to retrieve the dead vermin from the side of the road, a discussion on hygiene took place and it was decided that a pair of gloves was in order. No one had gloves in the car, but the folks working at the local Subway sandwich shop always wore gloves when they made sandwiches.

"I'll take a foot-long ham and cheese on rye, a bag of chips, a coke and a pair of those gloves," Jack's friend said, pointing to the Subway employee's clear plastic gloves.

"A pair of gloves?" the guy questioned, never having had someone order a pair with their foot-long.

"Yeah, an extra pair or two of those gloves. Don't ask," Jack's friend said, smiling at the guy.

A quick drive back to the abandoned stretch of highway to retrieve the beast was made. Jack's friend doubled up on gloves and they placed its carcass in a garbage bag. With the windows down, they drove into Damascus and parked the car as close to Jack's tent as they could get. No one was around, including Jack, and it was a fairly painless process to get into Jack's tent unnoticed.

"Good Lord his tent smells worse than this dead possum," Jack's friend said as he unzipped the nylon door and stuck his head in. They dumped out all of the stuff in Jack's backpack to make room for the road kill. And then they dumped in the possum, cinched the top, zipped up the tent door and walked away.

Jack was off milling around and catching up with folks at Trail Days. He got back to his tent late in the afternoon and didn't notice anything awry. His tent smelled, but he assumed it was just accumulated miles of hiker funk. He went back out and partied with an assortment of degenerate hikers late into the night. At some point in the wee hours, Jack came back to his tent and passed out.

And at some point early the next morning, he woke up and realized something horrible had taken place based on the bouquet in his tent. Initially he couldn't figure out what was happening. He opened the tent door and stuck his head out to look around. The air smelled much, much better outside the tent. He stuck his head back in and realized that, yes, the horrendous smell was in fact coming from inside the tent. He opened his backpack to find a dead animal in the initial throes of decomposition.

I asked Jack what he did next. "I took my pack to the local carwash and I spent the better part of an hour using the high pressure wand to hose it out," Jack relayed.

"What did you do with the possum?" I asked.

"I dumped it into the trash can beside the car wash vacuum. Some little old lady probably drove up to vacuum out her car and had half a coronary when she peered into that wretched trash can," he said with a hopeful laugh.

~ ~ ~

The oldest trick in the hiker trick book is to stealthily place rocks in someone's pack when they aren't looking. It's happened to me and to many hikers that have walked long trails. It almost feels like it has become some ridiculous right of passage. There is nothing worse (well, maybe a dead animal being placed in your backpack) than having just completed a 2,000 foot climb in the hot sun to find that someone added a couple pounds of rocks to your pack to make the already difficult even more so.

In 2004 on the PCT someone found the bottom third of a 5-iron off the side of the trail. It's unclear why a portion of a golf club would be found on the Pacific Crest Trail many miles from the nearest golf course, but that's what happened. I'm not sure who initially found it, but it eventually made it's way into my backpack and into many of the backpacks of the PCT Class of 2004.

By the time it found itself in my backpack, it came complete with a small notebook that contained an even smaller coin purse and picture of David Hasselhoff. The entire lot weighed close to a pound. I signed the notebook and immediately snuck it into my friend Strut's backpack while she was off taking a bathroom break near McIver Cabin one day.

Eventually the 5-iron made its way back into my backpack without my knowing and, when I did find it again for the second time, I decided I'd hike with it for a while. The change purse had grown and I figured I was rich now. I made sure to let other hikers know that I was in possession of the 5-iron to put fear in their hearts. Having the 5-iron gave me all the power.

I kept it with me for almost two weeks and some 200+ miles. It was a new record for the 5-iron and, at some point while taking a day off in Mojave, California, I bid it farewell and slipped it into my friend Salamander's backpack. She carried it for over 250 miles and I lost track of it after that.

Later that fall after the hike was over, I got to wondering about the 5-iron and I posted on a PCT forum inquiring about it. I got an email from Crazy John who apparently carried the damn thing 300 miles from Kennedy Meadows to Belden through the High Sierra. It then made its way via a few different hikers through northern California and southern Oregon. A hiker named Quasimoto contacted me with photographic evidence showing his friend Dr. Strog discovering the 5-iron in the bottom of his pack. Apparently Dr. Strog had unknowingly carried the 5-iron 250 miles to the town of Cascade Locks on the Oregon-Washington border. Dr. Strog was not happy at this discovery but then became giddy as he slipped it into the pack of a hiker he had just met.

It's lost on me how someone could hike for two weeks without knowing that a pound's worth of 5-iron, notebook, coin purse and Hasselhoff glamour shot had made its way into their backpack. I take almost everything out of my pack at night when I'm getting ready to call it a day. Both times I ended up with the 5-iron, I knew within a half a day. Dr. Strog had it for two weeks and didn't know it. Maybe it's better that way?

Again I would submit that boredom may be the biggest danger to hikers out there. Boredom causes all kinds of unwanted side effects: bad trail names, forest ninjas, missing shoes, unnecessary snow struggles, hacksawed hiking poles, packs full of dead animal, and golf clubs. Be careful out there.... it's a dangerous world.

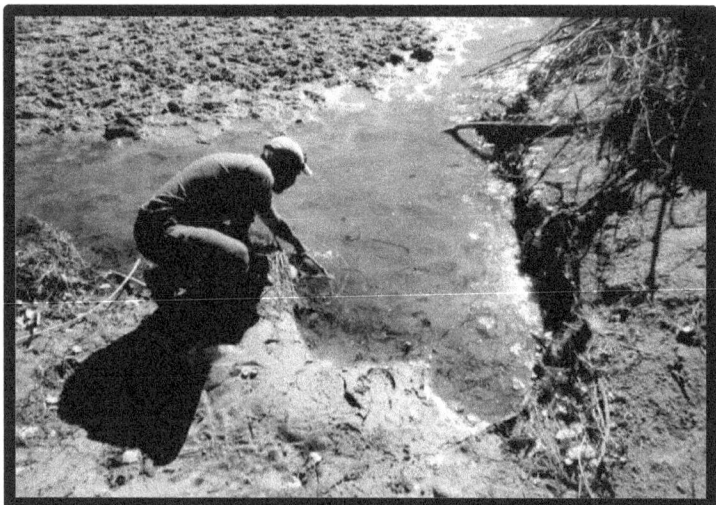

7

The Taste of Water

"You'll be fine. You could hike seven miles in the morning with your eyes closed," Honolulu said casually as we discussed my lack of water.

We had just finished the short climb up Stony Mountain in the infamous "Pennsylvania Rocks" section of the Appalachian Trail. The PA Rocks are a notorious segment of trail complete with long dry stretches between water sources, a plethora of rattlesnakes and small pointy and unforgiving rocks in the middle of the trail that make the going slow and the feet unhappy.

For the first time in as long as I could remember, I would go to bed thirsty without access to water. I desperately searched around the mostly rock-free dry creek bed where Honolulu, JC and I were camped for a spring, creek, puddle, something.... anything that might have a splash of water that I could filter. There was nothing. Dry as a bone. I had underestimated the June heat and how zapped this climb would leave me at the end of another 20-mile day.

My Appalachian Trail data book informed me that sure water would not be found for another seven miles at Rausch Gap Shelter and then a quarter-mile off a side trail from the shelter. My water bottle was a quarter full and the sun had already gone down. It was 8 p.m. and, even if I got up early, it would likely be at least 12 hours until I got to that water source at Rausch Gap. Honolulu said I could do the hike tomorrow morning in my sleep. I wasn't so sure.

~ ~ ~

The thing about water is that 99.9% of most everyday we think nothing of it. It's always there. I walk twenty feet into the kitchen, lift the handle on the faucet and like magic it appears, clear and cold as it funnels into a glass for as much as I can drink. Most of us in the developed world take something as fundamental as water for granted. We use it to wash our cars, water the lawn, water the garden, and water ourselves as we take our morning showers. It's a rare occasion that we go wanting for water.

Periodically we might find our town is "blowing out the pipes" and what is normally cold and clear turns a rusty orange for a few hours. We make do and by late afternoon it's cold and clear again and we forget that we were ever inconvenienced by having to go without. As of late, we've all heard about the folks in Flint, Michigan, that were unknowingly drinking tap water that was cold, clear and contaminated with high levels of lead and other toxins. Apparently this was a result of the city of Flint changing the source of their city's drinking water in 2014 to the

Flint River. It was only in 2016 that the red flag was officially raised and a federal state of emergency was declared.... and only after 100,000 residents were potentially exposed. Folks living in Flint have been instructed to continue drinking bottled water until 2020 when all of the lead pipes will have been replaced. That's hard to imagine for most all of us that don't live in Flint.

Even more extreme is Cape Town, South Africa. It's a major coastal city of four million people. And it's the first major city that is about to run out of fresh water. Completely out of water. City planners have even calculated the day this will happen. They are calling it "Day Zero." Originally Day Zero was calculated to be April 16th, 2018, and then was pushed to May and now to 2019 thanks to some much needed summer rains. Cape Town's dire situation is the result of years of persistent drought that have led to its reservoirs dropping to dangerously low levels never seen before. Residents have been rationed from 87 liters per person per day to 50 liters to 25 liters. Lines of Cape Town residents have already formed at community water faucets and local springs as armed guards stand by to make sure no one collects more than 25 liters a day. Think about that.

~ ~ ~

I was up at 6 a.m. and decided to wait on eating my breakfast of a single pre-wrapped energy bar as I had nothing to wash it down with. The few sips I had left in my water bottle had been consumed sometime around 3 a.m. when I woke up from a strange dream. I had dreamt that I was at an outdoor restaurant and, when the waiter came by to fill our water glasses, he only put a splash of H2O in each. He said they were almost out of water and that's all they had for each of us. Apparently my real world thirst had led to my dream world anxiety. I woke up and gulped down the few scant ounces of water I had left without considering I might want to take a drink on the seven-mile hike to Rausch Gap.

Honolulu and JC were also up and rustling about. I felt uneasy about asking them for some of their water as they also had been low when we got to camp the previous night. I packed up and walked out, hoping that I could in fact sleep walk all the way to the next water source.

The water at Rausch Gap was cold, clear and delicious. I drank deeply. Two liters were downed before I hiked out with another two liters in my backpack. I'm not sure what I would have done if the water at Rausch had been non-existent or too difficult to locate. I was glad I didn't have to think about that. The incident at Rausch led me to carry eight liters out of Scissors Crossing on the Pacific Crest Trail five years later in 2004.

~~~

The southern California section of the Pacific Crest Trail is approximately 650 miles long and runs from the Mexican Border to Kennedy Meadows on the south end of the High Sierra. Most hikers refer to this as the "desert" section of the PCT, but it's not desert in the likeness of the *Lawrence of Arabia* desert. It's actually a mix of high desert complete with all types of thorny plants, followed by a brief high elevation mountain range and then back down to desert.

The stretch of trail leading out of Scissor's Crossing traverses the dry and sun-scorched San Felipe Hills. Our next sure water source was Barrel Spring some 24 miles distant. I walked out of Scissors late afternoon with eight liters of water. At 2.2 pounds per liter that's 17 ½ pounds of water. You don't think about water.... I mean, really think about water until you've got 17 ½ pounds of it added onto the 25 pounds of stuff already in your backpack. Then you think about it a lot. You think about it every single strenuous step as you climb up 2,200 feet in elevation from the valley floor to the ridgeline as the unrelenting sun tries to drill a hole through the top of your head like a laser beam.

Long water carries became the norm in SoCal on the Pacific Crest Trail in 2004. I began to realize how precious this stuff really was when I was forced to load up with liter after liter due to the distance between reliable water sources. I began to think of myself as less of a backpacker and more of a mule that carried water and food from one far-off location to another. I also began to lower my standards.

A number of folks had taken to placing caches of one-gallon jugs of water near road crossings along the PCT. We had some dated information from the web that told us where these locations were. After getting burned early on by an empty cache that we were relying on for water, we had vowed not to rely on them again. We'd treat them as bonus water if, in fact, there was any water left in them after the pile of Pacific Crest Trail hikers making their way north along the trail had already gone through. The end result was a heavy pack as we carried all the water we'd need from one reliable (read non-water cache) source to the next. And periodically we'd happen upon a natural water source that wasn't in any of our guidebooks or water data.

Drinking water from a stagnant wetland isn't ideal. It's something I wouldn't even consider in my normal life. And why would I? There are three water faucets in my house and clean water in most every building in the town where I live. But on trail you take what you can get, and sometimes what you can get is a light brown tannin-filled liquid nestled amongst the reeds of a small wetland just off the side of the trail.

"Tastes like salad," my hiking partner said matter of factly. I proceeded to watch him down half of the liquid in his plastic bottle. I figured I should do the same. Indeed.... it tasted like salad.

I would have killed for some of that Pacific Crest Trail "salad water" when faced with some grim decisions on the Hayduke Trail. The Hayduke is a gem and a beast of a trail located in southern Utah and northern Arizona. It starts nondescriptly in Arches National Park and makes it way across public land as it traverses through Capitol Reef National Park, Bryce Canyon National Park, Grand Canyon National Park and finally ending in Zion National

Park. More of a route than a trail, the Hayduke is remote in location and desolate in feel. It's also quite dry. 20-mile water carries are the norm with a few 30-40 mile carries peppered in for good measure. As a Hayduke Trail hiker, you are a water carrier. Water becomes the thing you plan your days, nights, weeks and ibuprofen supply around.

I had never heard of alkaline water until I joined my good friends Skittles and Buck-30 for a 110-mile stretch of the HDT between Hanksville and Escalante. This stretch of the Hayduke shared a lot of trail tread with the many cattle that are routinely grazed for pennies on the dollar on BLM land. It also traversed the Henry Mountains, which topped out at 11,200' – the high point of the Hayduke Trail.

Pure unfettered water has a pH of 7. Generally speaking, water with a pH lower than 7 is considered acidic while water with a pH higher than 7 is considered basic (or alkaline). pH for most normal groundwater is roughly between 6-8.5, which is right around neutral and doesn't affect the water's taste. The alkaline water sources found along the Hayduke Trail had pH's higher than 8.5. Some as high as 12-14 and I can tell you for a fact that water with a pH that high tastes oddly bitter and repulsive.

Typically we knew if a water source was alkaline just by laying eyes on it. That characteristic chalky residue was evident as a white ring around the circumference of the surface of water source after water source. Alkali minerals in the soil in the form of calcium carbonate and sodium carbonate are the culprits. The water itself typically looks clear and appetizing until it hits your tongue. Most of the times it's palatable, but I found myself having to force it down. There is nothing quite like the last few sips of tepid alkaline water from an almost empty water bottle that has been basking in the afternoon sun on the side of my backpack.

There's also stomach distress. Some folks don't have much of any kind of reaction to alkaline water. Heck, it's even become a multi-million dollar subsection of the bottled water industry. A number of water companies and health gurus claim that drinking alkaline water can do wonders in restoring the body's pH balance and reducing acid reflux, high blood pressure, diabetes and high cholesterol. You can purchase a liter of the stuff from your local hippy grocer for $2.99 a bottle. I met a guy in Maui a few years back who had purchased a fancy water alkalizer so that he could take spring water and make it alkaline. He told me that he felt the healthiest he'd ever been in his life. Granted, the high dollar alkaline water from the hippy grocer and the water my Maui acquaintance was chugging down were just slightly higher in pH than tap water – between 8.5 and 9 pH. It wasn't anywhere close to being as revolting as the water I was pulling from most every source on the Hayduke.

Back to stomach distress. One of the side effects of having an excess of alkalinity in the body is gastrointestinal issues. The guidebook we had even warned of it. I didn't really believe it.... it's just water, right? By our third day of pulling water from little pools with chalky residue on the rims, I found that within about ten minutes of chugging a liter, I'd need to pull over and dig a hole. Over time I learned that sipping versus chugging alleviated most of the gastrointestinal distress.

The alkaline water on the Hayduke wasn't the only problem we had to contend with out there. The three of us were taking an alternate route up Silver Creek to avoid Hole in the Rock Road. Hole in the Rock Road is a desolate two-lane dirt surface that is some 30 miles from the town of Escalante – our next resupply point. It's also seldom traveled and apparently not a great place from which to hitch a ride. Our friends "Speedo" and "Nacho" had reached Hole in the Rock Road and spent over 24 hours with their thumbs out to no avail. They were out of food, out of water and out of luck as no one would give them a ride. Someone eventually had mercy on them and took them into town, but we weren't looking for a repeat of their experience.

The alternate up Silver Creek eventually led to a series of dirt roads that intersected with the paved road into Escalante. No hitching required. That worked for us and Silver Creek was only ankle deep at the most. The cold water felt refreshing on our feet and the hike through this section of red rock country was quite nice. The added bonus was not having to carry the standard five liters of water from an alkaline pool to get the 20 or so miles to the next. We had all the water we could possibly drink right below us and it wasn't alkaline.... it was great! I had just filled my water bottle and was taking a few swallows as we walked up on the motionless bull.

The bull was facing upstream away from us so we had a good view of his rear and the flies that had started to accumulate around him. At first I didn't know what I was looking at as I had never seen an animal stuck in quicksand.

"Look at that bull," I said to Skittles. "I think he's given up the ghost."

"Quicksand," Skittles said as we all immediately scurried out of Silver Creek and up onto a sandy willow-choked bank. We took a wide berth around the bull and at some point stopped again to take a hard look at his predicament.

Quicksand is formed when water saturates an area of loose sand. When the water trapped in the loose sand can't escape, it liquefies the area and that ground can no longer support weight. Often that happens on the sides of sandy riverbanks and can appear as solid ground. Once someone or something steps onto this saturated ground, the wet sand is agitated, liquefies, and then gives way. You step onto a liquid, you sink. When that 2,000 pound bull stepped onto that quicksand, it sank up to its neck. And then it died. I looked at my water bottle. It was full of water I had just filled from 100 yards downstream of the bull. I poured the rest of my water out and tried not to dwell on the half-liter I had just ingested.

At some point further upstream we ran into a Bureau of Land Management ranger on horseback who told us he had reports of a dead bull and asked if we had seen it. We gave him directions and suggested he fill his water bottles upstream.

Eventually Silver Creek dwindled to a thin ribbon of shallow, slow-moving water. Not wanting to carry any more water than we had to, we kept walking without filling our bottles. The closer we got to Escalante, the less water we'd have to camel into town. It had been half a mile or so since our stream had disappeared, but our maps told us we should find a little more water before the final 20-mile dry stretch into town. We popped out of Glen Canyon National Recreation Area into a sandy area with low riverbanks. I could see sun reflecting off the water's surface up ahead! My initial elation at having found more water was quickly tempered by the water source itself. It was a shallow, stagnant pool with a slightly oily sheen. There were hundreds of hoof prints along the water's edge and dozens of cow pies both on the banks and resting just under the surface.

"There's cow shit in the water," I said exasperated at what I was seeing.

"You'll be fine. It builds character," Buck-30 said, crouching down to fill four one-liter water bottles.

"You guys are really going to drink that?" I asked Skittles who was digging through his pack to find water bottles to fill.

"It's the last water for 20 miles. No choice," Skittles offered, as he found a spot to dip his bottle into.

I looked again at the water. There was cow shit everywhere. The last ribbon of flowing Silver Creek was a half-mile back. That's a 20 minute round trip. Aarrgghh!

Since Skittles and Buck-30 were getting water there, I surmised I probably should, too. I reluctantly reached for the empty water bladders in my backpack and walked over to the far edge of the pool. I determined that pulling water from the spot where the cow shit was four feet away from my bottle was better than pulling water from the spot where the cow shit was two feet away from my bottle. I gently dipped my bottle in, careful not to disturb the sand on the bottom of the pool. I methodically transferred water back and forth from the cow pool to my water bladders after first running it through a filter. Although I had confidence in my filter, I was really rolling the dice here given the obvious patties all around and within this dingy water source.

I pulled out a small Ziploc containing an emergency stash of chlorine dioxide drops. I figured this was somewhat of an emergency and treated all four liters with this bleach-like solution. The instructions on the side of the bottle recommended waiting 20 minutes after treatment before drinking. I waited an hour before taking that first sip.

I eyed both Skittles and Buck-30 taking swigs off their water bottles. "Tastes fine," Buck-30 offered, as he took a rather large swallow from his bottle. I didn't trust these guys. On many occasions I had seen both of them drink untreated water directly out of streams, ponds, springs, and a host of other more questionable water sources. I had seen my friends D-Low and Mags do the same many a time. They were all of the mentality that, if you drink enough untreated water, your system gets used to it and you can build up a resistance of sorts to the various gribblies that tend to call untreated water home. And even though Buck-30 and Skittles had both treated this poop water, I was still quite reluctant. I mean come on.... it's a repulsive thing to drink water that has been mixed with the shit of another animal. I was willing to let a lot of things slide in terms of hygiene on this eight-day hike with Skittles and Buck-30, but at no point during the previous weeks while preparing for this trip did I believe I'd be hoisting a pint of tepid turd water.

I gingerly put the lip of my water bottle to my mouth and took a small sip. I had filtered it and then treated it with chlorine. The taste.... well it tasted a bit like.... water.

By the time we walked the road shoulder into the dusty wayside that is Escalante, Utah, I had about eight ounces of room temperature liquid left in my last water bottle. I had taken to adding a bit of Emergen-C (an orange flavored vitamin/electrolyte powder) to make my cow water taste slightly more acceptable. It mostly worked as long as I didn't think too much about it. Amazingly enough I never got sick. Neither did Buck-30 or Skittles.

~~~

Outside of alkaline water and cattle-molested water, desert trails can present other problems when it comes to this #1 item in keeping a hike going and a body alive.

Deserts are dry by definition. As a result, water sources can be miles and miles apart. As mentioned earlier, water is heavy and typically long-distance hikers don't carry any more than they need to. Operating like this involves hedging one's bets that the next water stop will, in fact, have water.

I had shot a few air balls at water sources over the years. Back in 2006 as P.O.D., Skittles and I were hiking the Continental Divide Trail in northern New Mexico, we had hiked eight miles to a water trough only to find it contained a half-inch of rusty brown water and a standpipe with an open faucet. Apparently someone had forgotten to turn off the faucet and, as a result, whatever water was being pumped up from below ground was no more. It was a long, thirsty walk another eight miles to the next water trough that, luckily for us, had water in its standpipe.

Water sources in the desert aren't sure bets even when there is water. They are a seductive mistress that can break your heart and leave you high and dry. There was the small water trough that had water along with a dead crow floating in it. We passed on that one. And there was also the odd water trough that was full to the brim with cold clear water and thousands of tiny red worms wriggling around every inch of its space. I stared at that trough in mild repulsion and disengaged apprehension as I watched the worms cavort. I passed on that water source too.

In the spring of 2017 I was out hiking as much of the Arizona Trail as I could possibly get done in the 30 days I had available. I started the Arizona Trail on March 1st with two hiking buddies. I met "Haddock" while hiking the Te Araroa in New Zealand the previous year. "Thumbs Up" and I go way back to the Pacific Crest Trail in 2008. We dealt with a harrowing crossing of Kerrick Creek in Yosemite National Park during peak snowmelt and runoff that I'll never forget.

Haddock bailed early on Day 5 due to the disaster that had become of his feet. More than a dozen blisters made his toes look like raw hamburger on Day 3. He trudged along in constant pain until he came to his senses on Day 5 and called it good. Apparently he had spent the previous month in Indonesia wearing nothing but flip-flops every day, which had led to swollen feet. His regular hiking shoes were now too small for his oversized feet.

Thumbs up and I continued on and I lost track of the distance between the day's water sources as Haddock's departure had thrown me for a loop. By the time the afternoon sun was relenting and the shadows had become longer, I realized that our next water source was still three miles distant and I had only about a quarter-liter of water left.

Thumbs Up and I discussed the situation as he was also low on water. The water data we used ranked water sources from 0-4. 0 was not reliable, 1 was seasonal or "iffy," 2 was probable, 3 was fairly reliable, and 4 was a definite source. So far even the water sources that were ranked 2 or 3 had been flowing, due to a fairly wet winter in southern Arizona. The metal cattle trough three miles up the trail was ranked 2/3 and the notation beside the ranking said "trough full with some algae."

It didn't sound appetizing, but it did sound doable. The next sure bet water source wasn't for another 14 miles with some iffy water sources scattered in between. The comments for some of those iffy sources read: "low, murky with cattle, dead fish."

A full cattle trough with some algae was more preferable than a stock tank with dead fish that might not even have water. Onward to the cattle trough we marched.

We had roughly an hour of sunlight remaining by the time we arrived at the defunct corral that contained our water source. As I came down, the hill I saw a handful of desiccated railroad ties scattered about, a half-dozen ten-foot lengths of PVC pipe, a water trough, a large holding tank and a fenced enclosure that contained a water pump near the ground's surface. Thumbs Up and I walked over to the cattle trough and peered in. It looked like an abandoned terrarium.

The cattle trough was about half-full of a reddish-brown sludge, a host of aquatic-looking plants and a fair number of bugs swimming about. "Looks grim," I mentioned to Thumbs Up as we contemplated how quickly our filters would clog if this water got anywhere near them.

The two of us immediately went into problem-solving mode. We were both down to the last few sips of water in our bottles and had less than an hour before it got dark. We had 14 miles to our next sure water source and both of us were hungry and ready to cook dinner. No water equals no dinner. What to do?

Thumbs Up scurried over to the water pump. His movement shook me from the immobilized stare I had been giving to the bugs swimming around the cattle trough. I checked out the PVC pipes lying about and had a quick flashback to an odd situation in which Skittles and I found ourselves on the Grand Enchantment Trail back in 2014.

Skittles and I had hiked into a water source with empty bottles only to find the holding tank dry and the windmill that was supposed to be filling it in disrepair. There was a jury-rigged motor on a couple of planks of wood over a well that contained water roughly ten feet below ground. We could see the water, but had no way to get to it. We tried starting the motor that was connected to a pipe for siphoning the water up and into our bottles. We couldn't get it to work.

I had been carrying a 20 ounce plastic bottle used for mixing powdered drinks and I also had a few thick rubber bands. A few days earlier Skittles and I had attached the plastic bottle to the end of one of my trekking poles with the rubber bands to "fish" for water at another problematic source. That source contained water in a short well that was about four feet below the surface. It was a bit too far down for my arm to reach, even when lying flat on my stomach, but within grasp of the length of my trekking pole. We fished water out of that well 20 ounces at a time until each of us had four liters, enough to make it to the next source.

As we peered 10 feet down into the well, I knew my trekking pole would not be long enough to reach the surface of the water. But the PVC pipes lying around would! We attached the plastic bottle to one end of the 10-foot long pipe and fed it down the side of the well until it dipped into the cold clear water. Again, 20 ounces at a time, we filled up four liters each and hiked on.

Back to the predicament Thumbs Up and I were in. We had a cattle trough that look like a deserted fish aquarium and a large holding tank. Thumbs Up had checked out the nearby water pump and it was gated off and inaccessible. I eyed the PVC pipe and determined it would be of no help as there was no well.

I walked over to the large holding tank. It was about ten feet tall and six feet in diameter. There was a metal pipe jutting out from the base of it, going into and then popping out of the ground some twenty feet away to feed the cattle trough. There was also a skinny one-inch metal pipe coming out of the ground and running up to the top of the tank, hooking over the top and into the tank. I knocked on the side of the tank and it didn't make the echo typical of empty water tanks. "You think there's water in here?" I asked Thumbs Up.

"Hard to say unless we can get up there to look in," Thumbs Up replied.

About four feet up the side of the holding tank was a large metal nut that had been painted over. It was big enough that I guessed it would hold my weight if I could figure out a way to stand on it. The metal pipe coming out of the base of the tank was roughly a foot off the ground. I put my left foot on it and then my right foot on the metal nut and pushed myself up to a standing position. Thumbs Up came over to brace me. I wasn't quite tall enough to see in. I was close, though. I put both hands over the half-inch thick metal lip at the top of the tank and hoisted myself up far enough that I could look in.

It's as if God himself shined a light down from the heavens onto the sight set before me. That ten foot by six foot holding tank was 99% full with clear cold water. I shouted a few expletives and Thumbs Up grabbed his water bladders and handed them up to me. He stood under me and braced my left foot that was dangling in the air. It was just enough support to help me get my right arm up and over the metal lip of the tank. That metal lip was thin, somewhat sharp and unforgiving. Only about 20 seconds went by before it started digging into my armpit and hurting.

"I don't know how long I can hang on up here. The rim of this tank does not feel good on my armpit," I relayed to Thumbs down below.

151

"Hang on just a bit longer.... try and get those bladders filled," Thumbs said hopefully.

To complicate matters the soft-sided bladders he handed up to me are the dickens to fill in a situation where you are dipping them into a pool of water. The sides are soft and collapse in on themselves. I had to use my 20 ounce plastic bottle (I always carry at least one of these on every trip) to dip into the tank water and then manually fill up the soft-sided bladders.

I was able to get both bladders full before my armpit couldn't take anymore. I jumped down off the metal nut and onto the ground. We didn't quite have all the water we would need to last the night and the next 14 miles of hiking until the next reliable water source. I didn't think I could go back up to the lip of the tank and hang my arm over again as it was just too damn painful.

A brainstorming session ensued. It was getting dark and we didn't have much time left to figure things out. Earlier that day Thumbs Up had found a foam sit pad that had fallen off someone's backpack. He had considered leaving it but decided to pick it up and carry it with him, thinking he might run into its owner and be able to give it back later in the day.

"If you can drape this sit pad over the lip of the tank, it'll give your armpit some cushion," Thumbs Up said. I was standing with one foot on the decrepit railroad tie that was lying beside the cattle trough. It was about seven feet long. "I bet this will work too," Thumbs Up said as he motioned to grab the railroad tie.

That railroad tie looked as though it would crumble under the weight of a toddler. Pieces of the ends had already broken off, but oddly enough it was a lot more intact than it appeared. We leaned it up against the side of the tank near the metal nut. I gingerly climbed my way from the lower pipe to metal nut to railroad tie. I was hesitant at first, but it held my weight. I was able to reach over the top without having the metal rim bite into my armpit at all. "Yahtzee! We're in good shape!" I exclaimed to Thumbs Up. I spent the next few minutes manually transferring water from my plastic bottle to the three other water bladders I had taken up with me.

I laughed out loud as I poured the water. We had walked into what looked like an impossibly desperate situation and figured out a hair-brained way to make things work out. A bird flying over the area would have known all along that there was plenty of nice cold water in that holding tank. Most hikers had likely ignored the holding tank and walked down to the trough, looked in, shook their heads, considered their situation, and then walked on. We almost did the same but knew we needed something other than the slimy liquid in that cattle trough.

We hustled another quarter-mile down to a large oak tree and set up our shelters underneath its limbs just as night fell. I cooked dinner and had enough extra water to make a cup of tea. We both talked about how ridiculous but fantastic the day turned out.

8

Lost in Translation

La Vajol is a tiny town in Spain's Pyrenees Mountains, located within a stone's throw of the French border. The "trail" we were hikng, the GR11, followed a small two-lane highway into town. It was already hot at nine in the morning, and I knew that we had made a mistake.

We wandered into town searching for the font. Fonts, or water fountains, were usually centrally located in almost every Spanish town we had walked through thus far. By Day 5 we had come to depend upon them as a place to refill our water bottles, pour cold water on our heads, and find shade for a brief respite from the glaring July sun. The fonts were a godsend in the summer heat, and the one in La Vajol had a covered roof and space to relax. Best of all, no one else was there.

P.O.D. had tried her hardest to remain upbeat, but I was no longer able to fake it. We were barely five days into a three-week hike on the GR11, and it was obvious now that we were in Spain in the wrong month. It was also obvious that the "trail" we thought we'd be walking wasn't much of a trail at all. We would have known all of this ahead of time if we had actually done our due diligence when planning this hike.

~~~

"Maybe we should try a hike in Europe," I suggested. P.O.D. was only a month or so shy of finishing her graduate program at the University of Colorado and we were brainstorming ideas on a proper celebration. "We've never done any hiking together outside the US. You're fluent in Spanish. It might be a pretty cool way to see the Pyrenees," I suggested.

"The Camino is a road walk and crowded with gobs of people. We would hate it. There's a couple other hiking routes that avoid roads, are less crowded and stay higher in the mountains," I said as if I knew.

The Camino de Santiago, called "The Camino" for short, is a world famous footpath and pilgrimage that sees over 200,000 people a year attempt to walk its entire length. P.O.D. and I typically go on hikes to get away from the masses; 200,000 people didn't sound like a good fit for us.

We had also heard about the HRP, a.k.a. the Haute Randonnée Pyrénéenne or High Route Pyrenees. And we had heard some of this 500-mile route from the Mediterranean Sea to Atlantic Ocean involved rock climbing so we wrote it off thinking it was a bit out of our league.

ر

The happy middle was supposed to be the GR11 (Grand Randonee 11), which is slightly lower in elevation than the HRP, but still higher than the Camino, and non-technical. The "GR" footpaths traverse land all over Europe. France alone has over 37,000 miles of GR footpaths. Belgium, the Netherlands, Spain and other European countries also contain GR footpaths.

The bulk of the diminutive research I had done on the GR11 involved quickly perusing Wikipedia, ordering a single guidebook, and reading a few online articles about the trail. I think all told I spent about five hours researching the hike and about one hour assembling my gear. P.O.D. had no time to do research as she was in the final throes of her last semester of grad school in addition to holding down a full-time job.

I had become complacent at planning hiking trips by the time our Spain adventure rolled around in 2012. I had done four 2,000+ mile hikes on long trails in the United States. I couldn't imagine that hiking in Spain or anywhere else in Europe would be much different. I was wrong.

The first hiccup we encountered concerned the box of gear we mailed to our friend Manuel in Barcelona. We had taken to only flying with carry-ons to avoid lost baggage and to get out of airports more quickly and efficiently. We were also averse to paying the various checked bag fees that had become the norm on most airlines. That box of gear contained all the stuff we thought TSA wouldn't let us carry on a plane: pocket knives, camp stove, trekking poles, tent stakes, etc.

We assumed that the airline charged for checked bags. We assumed this without actually checking. Only after we paid $65 in postage to mail our box to Barcelona, did I find out that checked bags were free. Ugh. I rationalized it as being ok overall as we'd be able to get in and out of the airport more quickly, not having to deal with checked bags.

I had been checking the tracking number on our box of gear and noticed it had been sitting in the Canary Islands for a few days without moving. P.O.D. made some phone calls and determined that our box had been red flagged for containing "undocumented sporting goods." Apparently Spanish customs thought that we were trying to sneak sporting goods into the country to sell on the black market and avoid taxes. I laughed at this notion because everything in that box was well-used and wouldn't be worth much money. It took a few more calls to get the box out of the Canary Islands and into Spain.

Several days passed and the tracking number showed our box was now sitting in Madrid. More phone calls ensued. The customs folks in Madrid had red flagged the box once again. The Madrid folks also thought we were trying to sneak sporting goods into the country to sell on the black market. We reached out to our friend Manuel in Barcelona. Manuel was heading to Madrid for a business trip and assured us that he could get the box out of customs.

Unfortunately, showing up in person to the customs office in Madrid wasn't enough to prove that he was not a reseller of used sporting goods. Customs would not give Manuel the box. They told him that another official would have to come in and investigate the situation. That official was on leave until the following week.

By the time we landed in Barcelona, the box of gear was still in Madrid and the situation was still up in the air. We spent a few extra days at Manuel's flat, hoping that our box would clear customs and arrive before we started the hike. By our third day in Barcelona, we lost hope and decided Plan B was in order. Manuel had two pairs of old ski poles and we went out and bought duplicates of most of the rest of the stuff in the box: pocket knives, tent stakes, a stove, etc.

The following morning we took a train from the center of the city to the northern coast to start the hike. Our box arrived at Manuel's later that same day.

~~~

A young hiker who was wise beyond his years once said, "Get yourself to the trail, the rest will figure itself out." We took this mantra to heart as we walked the city trails from the town of Cadaques past the nude beach to Cap de Creus, the eastern terminus of the GR11. The past few days left us a bit frazzled as did the train station in Barcelona. I can't tell you how thankful I am that P.O.D. is fluent in Spanish; even she had trouble figuring out the train schedules there. If it had just been me trying to make sense of it all, I'd still be in the Barcelona train station right now, standing there with my mouth agape. Habla ingles??

Neither one of us slept well that first night on the trail. We were crammed into some low bushes 50 yards off the main path. The night was warm and the adrenaline of all that had transpired on Day 1 hadn't worn off. It turned out that the bulk of the GR11 during those first few days headed west from the Mediterranean Sea as a fairly shadeless affair in the low scrub of the coastal foothills. Our "trail" was a mix of wide dirt paths, rough dirt roads, smooth dirt roads and paved roads. Shade from the July sun was rare and we found ourselves raising our trusty silver umbrellas almost immediately.

By the time we walked the paved road into La Vajol, it was evident that the GR11 was not going to be a remote hike in the forest. The abundance of roads and towns that we had already hiked through would become the norm. And the daytime temps left us sluggish and lacking of energy. If I had done any real research and legitimate planning, I would have known that Spain in July is a caldron. Hindsight is 20/20, I suppose, and here we were in La Vajol, Spain, on an unbearably hot day, walking paved road shoulders. What to do?

"This trail sucks," I said to P.O.D. as we sat under the roof of the town's font. There was a short silence, then P.O.D. said matter of factly, "Well, we're here and I don't know what to tell you."

"How are we going to spend another two weeks hiking through this heat?" I asked P.O.D. somewhat pathetically. "I don't know, but we're going to have to figure something out," she said.

Over the course of the next few hours we drank copious amounts of water and discussed our options. The first thing we ruled out was quitting the hike. We didn't have a lot of money and the cheapest possible way to spend 21 days in Spain was to hike while avoiding nights and expensive meals in towns. There was no other possible way to spend our remaining weeks in Spain more cheaply than hiking, and we didn't want to go sit in our friend's apartment for the next three weeks and I'm sure he would have felt the same.

We discussed and debated and decided that we would abandon our plan to hike 350 miles of the 522-mile trail. We had surmised that we could do 350 miles by hiking 20 miles a day and only taking a few days off here and there. We were struggling to get in 20 miles each day but had been forcing ourselves to do so in order to stick to "the schedule." We decided to throw out the schedule altogether and take the rest of the day off in the cool shade by the font. Immediately our moods got better as did our outlooks on the remaining time we had left in Spain.

Ultimately we decided that we would switch to the siesta style of hiking we had employed on the Pacific Crest Trail in the desert section of southern California... and why not, Spain originated the siesta! Some of the hottest days

PCT thru-hikers encounter are in May, which is when the bulk of hikers are heading north through southern California. Typically the hottest part of the day is between noon and 5 p.m. On really hot days it's counter-productive to try to hike between noon and 5 p.m. unless, of course, you are trying to stick to "the schedule" or you hate yourself or you take particular pleasure in feeling miserable.

Most PCT hikers that weren't into those types of things would embrace the siesta. You hit the trail around 5 a.m. and hike until noon. Noon to five is spent under the shade of an oak, or pine, or Joshua tree. The main meal of the day is consumed during this time and not much effort is exerted doing anything else. Just lying around in the shade biding time until the heat starts to subside. Then from 5 – 9 p.m. or so, you hike some more miles and get to enjoy one of the best parts of desert hiking - watching all the animals and birds come alive again at dusk. It's a truly magical time of day to be on trail.

Granted, the Pyrenees Mountains of Spain are not the same as the deserts of Southern California, but the heat demanded a similar hiking style. So the next day we found ourselves a shady spot and took noon to five off. It was wonderful. So wonderful that we took siesta every day for the rest of the trip. When in Spain, do like the Spaniards.

~ ~ ~

One thing we noticed was that our fellow European hikers were on a much different hike even though we were all sharing the same footpath. The Spaniards, in particular, were accustomed to the heat and would hike through midday. We arrived early one evening to the ruins of a long-abandoned castle and decided to set up camp nearby. I had on shorts and no shirt. P.O.D. had on shorts and a sports bra. We were both sweating profusely and thankful that the sun had started to finally bend behind the horizon. There were four Spaniards also camping nearby. All four of them had on fleece pants and jackets in addition to wool beanies. I looked at P.O.D. and she looked back at me. "How are they wearing all that fleece? It is actually hot, right?" I asked.

Most of the European hikers we met were carrying huge packs and were sleeping at hostels or *refugios* in town every night. We were doing the exact opposite. Hoping to save money and not that interested in sleeping indoors, we were camping out every night between towns. Incidentally, camping in the backcountry in Europe is called *Wild Camping*. I'm not sure what Europeans would call non-wild camping. Is that when you sleep in a bed but have the window open to your room? Or is it when you sleep in your car?? No clue.

The other thing about sleeping in towns is that most European hikers would arrive in town during early afternoon and then leave late the next morning, forcing them to hike during the hottest part of the day. I suppose

I'd want to sleep in a bed every night, too, if I were marching up and down the Pyrenees Mountains in the July heat during the hottest part of the day everyday. It just didn't make sense to me. Why not adjust your hiking schedule to beat the heat? And why the insistence on sleeping under a roof every night? Weren't we all out here to enjoy our time outdoors?? Sleeping outside is one of the best parts of distance hiking. Sleeping indoors is for everyday life back at home.

We weren't complete vagabonds, however. We typically got a room at a hotel or hostel once a week or so to get a shower. When we'd mention that it had been a while since our last shower, we'd get odd looks of confusion from our European compatriots. "Where did you stay last night?" they would ask.

"We were camped in the woods," we'd respond.

"You were wild camping?" we'd be asked with a look of perplexed apprehension.

"Um, yeah. We were *wild camping*," we'd respond with a chuckle.

The reality is that the American hiking style is much different than the typical European hiking style. Most of Europe is more densely populated than the US. There aren't as many national forests, parks, Wilderness areas, and large expanses of woodlands in Europe. What hiking areas do exist in Europe are a bit more civilized. Staying in huts is the norm while trekking in Europe. The US is the exact opposite. 35% of mainland US is public land. We have huge expanses of forests and a truly remarkable system of long trails. Only one of the US long trails, the Appalachian Trail, has something akin to a "hut" system. And, even then, the 250 or so three-sided shelters on the AT would be considered "rustic" compared to the huts you find along trails in Europe. Hiking in Spain (and also in New Zealand) made me realize that we truly have something very unique and special here in the United States. There is no other place on Earth that has the amount of untrammeled forests and hiking trails that we do.

~~~

We were stopped one day by a Spaniard out for a day hike who asked us where we had stayed the night before. We told him that we had *wild camped* ten kilometers back. His eyes got big. He told us he was running low on water and asked us where we had gotten our water. We told him about an incredibly cold spring just five or so minutes back up the trail. "What is a spring?" he asked. P.O.D. and I stared at him blankly. Then P.O.D. told him that it's a place where water comes out of the rocks. "You drank water from the ground? It's untreated right?" he asked quizzically.

"We treated it with our water filter, but you could probably drink it straight as it looks really good," P.O.D. offered. "It's just five minutes up the trail. You'll see it to the left of the trail in a jumble of boulders."

"I'll be ok," the guy replied.

It was obvious he had no intentions of drinking water from the ground. And it was obvious he thought we were crazy to do so. He wasn't the only one. We found that most Europeans on the GR11 would carry enough water to get from one town to the next, passing up "water from the ground" on purpose. They all had water filters but used them only for emergency purposes. And to think folks in California are paying $30 a bottle for "raw water!"

Oh, the cigarettes! As a former smoker I still notice other smokers, especially smokers on trail. It seems mad to smoke while you are doing something (i.e. hiking) that involves extensive use of your cardiovascular system. It doesn't take a medical degree to realize that you are working against yourself if you smoke while you are out hiking. Smoking has also become less pervasive in the US. Smoking rates have declined significantly over the past two decades in God's Country. Apparently Europe didn't get the memo. Over half the Europeans we met on trail were smokers. One memorable day on an uphill, I watched a German guy laboring up the steep climb in the heat of the day. There was no shade anywhere and he stopped halfway up to have a smoke break in the sun. He still had the second half of the hill to climb. I shook my head and said hello as I hiked through the cloud of *Marlboro* smoke on my way around him. I was beginning to wonder if I truly was hiking the same trail as my fellow Europeans. I pinched myself. It hurt.

The biggest difference, though, had nothing to do with cigarettes, or water filters, or sleeping in beds. It had everything to do with the traditional roles that Spaniards still endure and the machismo that is still very much the norm in Spanish culture.

There is an old Spanish proverb that goes something like this: "La mujer en casa y el hombre en la plaza." It means that the woman stays in the house and the man stays outside. Spanish sayings like this one may be hundreds of years old, but the mentality still exists in modern day Spain. That's not to say that things are excellent here in the US. We know they are not. Inequality between the genders has been a problem since before the United States came into existence. But I will tell you that it's been a long, long time since I heard someone say to P.O.D., while we were hiking together on a US trail, "So did he drag you out here?" I always find that question completely ridiculous and laughable. The assumption, of course, being that because P.O.D. is a she, she would naturally have an aversion to being outdoors instead of doing domestic chores at home because that is what all women aspire to do. Good grief. Again, I've encountered this attitude in the US, but we encountered it almost daily while in Spain.

A few hours before we met the bewildered Spanish day hiker who was horrified that we were drinking water from a spring, we emerged above treeline for the first time on the GR11. We were traversing an alpine ridgeline in some incredible country. We were elated to be hiking on a true trail and not on dirt or paved roads. Just as quickly as we had become smitten with the Pyrenees, we started intersecting runners wearing race bibs. It turned out there was a trail race that Saturday originating out of a ski area just down the mountain. At first it was just a single runner here and there and we easily moved over to let them pass. Then it became a conga line of 20 or more runners at a clip. We decided to pull over and take an extended break to let all the runners go by.

There were a few spectators on the trail with cow bells cheering and shouting words of encouragement as the runners loped by. "¡Venga, Venga, Venga!" the onlookers shouted. I asked P.O.D. what they were shouting.

"It means come on - hurry up - go," P.O.D. replied.

And then she started shouting "¡Venga, Venga, Venga!" And then I started shouting "¡Venga, Venga, Venga!" We had a lot of fun that afternoon encouraging the runners on their way.

The gaggle of racers dissipated into a few small groups of two or three and then into a few solo runners here and there. We got up from our rest spot, shouldered our backpacks and got back on the trail. The final few runners we saw heading up as we headed down the mountain looked a bit worse for the wear.

We reached the base area of the ski resort to find a big party for the racers in full swing! There were huge tables of food, soda, beer, water, fruit and a live band filled the air.

"Holy moly," I said to P.O.D. "Look at all that food." I was eyeballing the large tables full of picnic-style food. And the buckets of beer. I looked around and most of the 200+ people were feasting.

"I'll be back," P.O.D. said. Five minutes later P.O.D. showed up with some sausages, chips and beer. To say I was elated is putting it mildly. We may not have been in the race that day but we helped cheer on the runners. Plus we had walked to this place from the Mediterranean Sea. Surely that was worthy of a sausage, chips and a *San Miguel*.

We lingered a bit at the party. "It's five o'clock. We need to hit the trail," I remarked, looking down at my watch. We still had a couple hours of hiking to get in before calling it a day.

Back on the trail with a full belly, the miles flew by. We were cruising quickly down the trail and had about an hour or so left before day turned to night. Our map showed a trailhead just up ahead and its contour lines looked spread out enough to presume there would be a flat spot for camping before we headed down to the next valley.

As we got within eyeshot of the trailhead, I spotted three older Spanish men at the trailhead parking lot. They took off their packs and set them down on the ground. Our trail took us down to the parking lot. "Buen dia," I said without skipping a beat or slowing down. "Buen dia. ¿A donde vas?" one of the Spaniards said to me. I didn't quite know what he had asked me as my Spanish was "fatal" back then.

"Lo siento, no habla Espanol," I replied. P.O.D. immediately chimed in, speaking in Spanish. I slowly kept hiking away from the parking lot to try to get P.O.D. to do the same. We had only a short amount of daylight at this point and needed to find a place to camp before dark.

I had walked to a point where the trail started to bend around the corner. I would have lost sight of P.O.D. if I had continued walking. I could see her still speaking with the three men. Ugh. I looked at my watch. I looked back at P.O.D. Still talking. I looked at my watch again and then I shouted, "¡Venga, Venga, Venga!" in P.O.D.'s direction. Immediately the Spanish guys started shouting back at me in angry voices. I had no idea what they were saying, but I could tell from their tone of voice that they weren't wishing me good health. A few seconds later P.O.D. broke away from them and hustled up to where I was standing. We rounded the corner and she started laughing. I could not figure out what was going on.

"What the heck did those guys say?" I asked P.O.D. as we hustled down the trail.

After I had said "Lo siento, no habla Espanol (I'm sorry, I don't speak Spanish), P.O.D. had chimed in, "Excuse me, do you guys know if there might be a campsite up ahead?"

"What? Camp? It's all trail that way," one of the men replied.

"Yes of course, but are there any spots to put up a tent?" P.O.D. retorted.

"You're thinking of sleeping out here?" one of the other Spaniards asked, concerned.

"Yeah, in our tent," P.O.D. offered starting to regret having asked about camping in the first place. We never actually told folks that we were sleeping under a tarp instead of a tent as the concept of tarp camping was pretty much unknown in Spain that we could discern and would raise all kinds of eyebrows.

"What are you doing here? Where are you from?" the puzzled Spaniard asked P.O.D.

"We're from Colorado and we're hiking on the GR11 for about three weeks," P.O.D. said.

The one Spaniard that had yet to speak chimed in, "You should be in the city, shopping!"

"Yes, why doesn't your husband take you to a spa or shopping or for a massage? What kind of man thinks of bringing his wife out here backpacking and sleeping in a tent?" one of the other men asked with a disapproving tone.

P.O.D. laughed. "'First of all, it was my idea…. and why can't I be here…. and shopping and hanging out in the city sounds mighty boring!"

"No, you're wrong…. your husband should treat you better," the man said, his blood pressure rising.

Right about this time I shouted "¡Venga, Venga, Venga!" which made the three Spaniards really distressed. That's when they started shouting curses at me in Spanish.

P.O.D. hastily bid them adieu and hurried up the trail to catch me and explained what had just happened.

"So they thought you should be in town shopping, huh?" I asked, shaking my head and laughing.

"Yeah, with their small brains they couldn't imagine that I would be out here hiking unless you had dragged me here against my will," P.O.D. said, shaking her head and laughing.

"¡Venga, Venga, Venga!" I shouted one last time before we found a nice flat spot off the side of the trail to set up our "tent" that evening.

"¡Venga, Venga, Venga!" P.O.D. shouted back.

9

Dog Days

Overmountain Shelter is an idyllic place to stop and take a break. It is a renovated barn just off the Appalachian Trail in the lonesome mountains of eastern Tennessee. It hosts a stunning view of a sublime valley down below and the Hump Mountains off in the distance. I stopped in for a quick rest and to elevate my throbbing feet.

I had just completed three big days and wasn't sure how much further I wanted to go. I pulled out my Appalachian Trail data book to scope the terrain ahead. There were a few folks milling about at Overmountain Shelter and I overheard some talk about fishhooks.

"One of the locals strung fishing line with fishhooks attached to it across the trail. They hate hikers," the grizzly-looking man lamented.

"They set fire to Apple House Shelter a few years back. They wanted to burn it down to send a message," the lady at his side blurted out.

I'd been hearing rumblings about the section of trail near Roan Mountain and Elk Park for about a week. The scuttlebutt on the trail was that the roughly 20 mile stretch between Apple House Shelter and Moreland Gap Shelter was not the friendliest stretch of the AT. Rumor had it that some of the locals didn't care for all the long hairs and dirty hippies that were showing up in their tiny towns during the spring. The Apple House Shelter in particular had a reputation as being a shelter to avoid, given its proximity to US Hwy 19 and the non-hikers, angry locals and homeless people that reportedly chose to pass time there.

The Apple House Shelter was only nine miles from Overmountain Shelter and I'd be there by late afternoon I guessed, glancing at my watch. If I pushed past the shelter, I'd be camping solo somewhere in the middle of this forbidden section of trail.

Sparky and Walrus walked in and sat down across from me. They pulled out a bag of trail snacks and commenced eating. Sparky and Walrus were an older couple from New Mexico. Apparently Walrus had been a minister, but you'd never know it by looking at him. He looked like any other bearded hiker out on the trail. We talked about the upcoming section of trail and he, too, had heard the warnings about Roan Mountain and Elk Park.

"We're camping at Doll Flats tonight and plan to push to Kincora tomorrow," Walrus said, with an ease I found welcoming. "If you're nervous about the next section, you should camp with us tonight and we'll hike through together tomorrow," he offered.

This changed everything. I felt he had just given me permission and a good reason to pump the brakes, throttle back and slow the miles. I could hike six miles and camp at Doll Flats, which was a few miles shy of Apple House Shelter, and then hike through the menacing section in one big push in the morning. My body needed a short day and it would be nice to set up my tent early and lounge around a bit.

~ ~ ~

Doll Flats is an unassuming piece of ground but, true to its name, it had a plethora of flat spots great for setting up a tent. The rest of the evening was uneventful minus my fumbling around with a set of extra batteries inside the tent that randomly sparked when touched together. I had vivid dreams that night and a restless sleep left me wide-awake just as the sun came up.

As early as I was up, Sparky and Walrus were up even earlier. They already had their backpacks on as I was getting out of my tent. "See you up the trail," Walrus said with a wave. "Yeah, see you in a bit," I said, a bit spooked. There's no doubt I had definitely let my mind wander in all sorts of terrible and unconstructive directions. Visions of fishhooks hanging down onto the trail and banjo playing locals saying "Where you goin' city boy?" danced in my head.

Two other hikers cruised through Doll Flats as I was getting ready to hike out that morning. Safety in numbers, I thought. There'd be at least five of us going through this section together.

Apple House Shelter was unremarkable. The three-sided small wooden cabin looked dingy inside. All manner of broken glass and half burnt tuna and Bud Light cans littered the fire pit. No one was there. I barely gave it more than a glance as I hustled by.

I caught Walrus, Sparky and the other folks just before crossing US Hwy 19 which served as the road into Roan Mountain, Tennessee, to the west and Elk Park, North Carolina, to the east. I definitely felt like we were behind enemy lines at this point. This was supposedly the epicenter of the anti-hiker sentiment in the area. Shortly after crossing the highway, the AT data book showed we'd also be crossing a series of local roads: Bear Branch Road, Buck Mountain Road, Campbell Hollow Road and Walnut Mountain Road. I had been hearing itinerant gunfire all morning (as you do) coming from the direction in which we were heading.

In addition to stories of fishhooks and arson, we had heard that the locals living near the section of trail over the next eight miles from the highway to Laurel Fork were especially upset about the AT because it ran so close to their properties. Some even said the trail crossed pieces of land that used to be their property. I had no way of knowing rumor from fact, but I did feel uncomfortable as we hiked within eyesight of various homes. I think every house between the highway and Laurel Fork that we passed in 1999 also contained a pit bull or a Rottweiler. For the most part, the dogs were chained up or behind a fence. They went nuts at the first sight of us and champed at the bit to run free and get a taste of hiker! How disappointed they'd be given how skinny most of us were.

I had paused to pull a snack out of my pack when Walrus and Sparky caught up to me.

"How you doing Disco?" Walrus said with a smile on his face.

"Alright I suppose. Ready to get through and get out of this section," I said with a bit of exasperation in my voice.

The next thing that happened is something that has never happened to me before or since in 15,000 miles of long-distance hiking.

"Let's say a prayer Disco," Walrus said, as he grabbed my hand and Sparky's hand.

I reactively grabbed Sparky's free hand and the three of us stood in a circle on the middle of the Appalachian Trail. Walrus closed his eyes and bowed his head.

"Dear Lord, please give us safe passage today as we walk on your trail. Please be with us every step of the way as we continue our journey north. Please be with Disco and put his mind at ease as he walks today. Please be with

Sparky and me and with all the hikers out here in your beautiful creation."

Walrus continued with the Lord's Prayer, "Our father who art in heaven, hallowed be thy name. Thy kingdom come, thy will be done. On Earth as it is in heaven. Give us this day our daily bread. Forgive us our debts as we forgive our debtors. Lead us not into temptation, but deliver us from evil. For thine is the kingdom, the power and the glory forever. Amen."

Sparky and I said "Amen" and I looked up and thanked Walrus. He smiled and said we'd all be at Kincora before we knew it. They hiked on and I finished eating my snack. I immediately felt better.

I hiked out and caught Sparky and Walrus right before the next road where we all caught the couple that had been in front of us for most of the morning. They were standing on the edge of the road where the trail crossed and looking a bit freaked out. There were two Rottweilers barking incessantly. Unfortunately for us, our trail followed the road for a quarter mile or so before ducking back into the woods. Those Rottweilers were absurdly large, angry and off-leash. And we had to get past them.

Walrus walked up front and started poking his hiking pole at the dogs and we tucked in right behind him. The five of us yelled and screamed at the dogs as they barked and growled at us. They followed us every step of the way over that quarter mile, lunging at us periodically. When the trail ducked back into the woods, they were still charging and snapping at us, but they did not follow us up the trail. As we rounded the bend I lost eyesight of them, but looked back over my shoulder frequently during the next half hour or so. I had visions of *Cujo* coming at me full throttle with teeth bared and ready for dinner.

Truth be told those Rottweilers could have made quick work of any of us. If it hadn't been for Walrus leading the way, we might all still be standing there on the edge of that rural road, afraid to go forward. I can't tell you how lucky I was as a newbie hiker out there on the AT in 1999 to have folks like Walrus and Sparky helping me along. We made it to Kincora Hiker Hostel later that day without any other issues. I've thought about those dogs many times since that day. Those were the biggest dogs I had ever encountered in almost 20 years of long-distance hiking.... except of course for the monster near Kokomo Pass.

~~~

Grazing animals on public lands have been part of the fabric of the American West since before you and I were born. Over the last century, 14 states spanning 250 million acres of public land in the western US have been host to thousands upon thousands of cattle, sheep, goats and horses. Many privately owned ranches don't contain enough land to host all these animals, so the ranchers pay Uncle Sam for the rights to use public land to graze them.

The herd of over 300 sheep grazing high above treeline near the Colorado Trail appeared bucolic. We had been hearing their constant bleating and chatter as we left Searle Pass headed for Kokomo Pass and Camp Hale beyond. They weren't actually that far from the trail.... perhaps only 50 or so feet below the path.

It's not uncommon for sheep to be grazed in Colorado's high country. I thought back to the various signs I had seen over the years imploring hikers to stay on the trail when above treeline so as not to injure sensitive alpine plants. I thought about those signs as I looked at this herd of 300 sheep trampling haphazardly over all manner of alpine tundra and "sensitive plants." I guess grazing animals don't count. Never mind that typical male sheep can weigh up to 350 pounds and their hooves are much rougher on the land than a pair of rubber-bottomed shoes. "It's ok, though," I said sarcastically to P.O.D., "It's our country's heritage, we don't need sensitive alpine plants anyway. We can't eat them."

The thing about large herds of sheep is that they are usually guarded by sheep dogs. The sheep dog of choice is the Pyrenees Mountain Dog or Great Pyrenees as we like to call them in North America. Great Pyrenees have been around for hundreds of years (possibly longer), having originated from the region around the Pyrenees Mountains in southern France and northern Spain. People who have them for pets typically describe them as gentle, fluffy and affectionate. The one we met between Searle and Kokomo Pass was anything but.

Most breeds of dogs have a specific purpose or had a specific purpose historically before they became pets. The smashed-face pug was originally used as a bed-warmer for British nobility. The golden retriever was used to retrieve ducks and pheasants shot during hunts in Europe. The loyal St. Bernard was used in the Swiss Alps as a search and rescue dog. Great Pyrenees are animal and livestock herding dogs and, when actually performing that task, they are very protective and can be anything but gentle and affectionate.

Great Pyrenees as herding dogs tend to patrol the perimeter of the flock. Their job is to defend the flock from coyotes, wolves or any other predator that may try to attack one of their sheep. They are very good at their job and by the looks of the 100+ pound Great Pyrenees that was now charging towards P.O.D. and me, we knew it thought we were trying to sneak into its herd to kill a sheep.

I immediately resisted my instinct to run. There's no way P.O.D. or I could have outrun this dog anyway and running has a way of triggering an animal's chase response. "Don't run," I said to P.O.D. as my voice broke. She was right behind me. I grabbed the pepper spray out of the side pocket of my backpack and calmly pointed it at the dog's face as it barked and bared its teeth at me.

The little canister of pepper spray I had with me was one of those that conveniently fits on a key chain because of its diminutive size. And because of its diminutive size and the dog's gargantuan size, I was reluctant to pull the trigger. I didn't think it would be enough to incapacitate a dog this big and thought it might just make him angrier.

Two more smaller dogs ran up and started barking at us, too. We slowly started backing up as I had the pepper spray still in my hand, desperately hoping I wouldn't have to use it.

"That's a good boy," P.O.D. said in a calm voice. I followed suit.

"You all are good boys, aren't ya. You're good dogs," I said, trying to convince them and myself at the same time.

The barking of the smaller two dogs decreased and one of them actually walked up to P.O.D. and started leaning against her leg looking for a pet. The Pyrenees had yet to relent, but he did temporarily stop lunging at us.

"I think we can keep backing up and then go way around them," I suggested, eyeing the wide-open tundra behind us. Pyrenees was still barking.

"Do you have any food?" I asked P.O.D.

"I've got some Wheat Thins in my side pocket," P.O.D. offered.

"Throw him some Wheat Thins and we'll keep backing up," I said with the pepper spray still pointed at his head, which appeared to be twice the size of mine.

"Hear ya go. That's a good boy," P.O.D. said in a soothing voice as she tossed a dozen crackers in front of the frothing beast.

He stopped barking and stuck his nose down to smell the crackers. And then he ate all of them. We had continued backing up and had put 20 feet or so between us and them. The two smaller dogs got bored and left. Pyrenees barked twice more and then turned around and walked back towards the flock.

The adrenaline stopped and immediately fear turned to anger. We were out here hiking a section of the Colorado Trail/Continental Divide Trail on public lands. No one should ever have their lives threatened or put in jeopardy by a rancher's privately-owned sheep dog while recreating on public lands. Someone is going to get hurt or worse I thought to myself as we hiked well off the trail and around the flock of sheep.

Just as we were about to reconnect with the Colorado Trail, we spotted the shepherd that was in charge of this flock. He was walking toward us. I was really pissed at this point.

"You need to control your damn dogs! They tried to bite us," I yelled at the guy. He looked back blankly without saying anything. "Your damn dogs are running around here off-leash. They're going to kill somebody."

The guy continued to look at us blankly, shrugged his shoulders, mumbled a few things and then turned around and walked back towards the flock.

His reaction seemed odd. The whole situation was perplexing and odd.

"Let's get the heck out of here," I said to P.O.D. as she stood there holding an empty Ziploc with a few Wheat Thin crumbs. At the next town stop in Leadville, I purchased a box of Wheat Thins. I ate most of them the first day out of town but kept an emergency stash in my hipbelt pocket just in case.

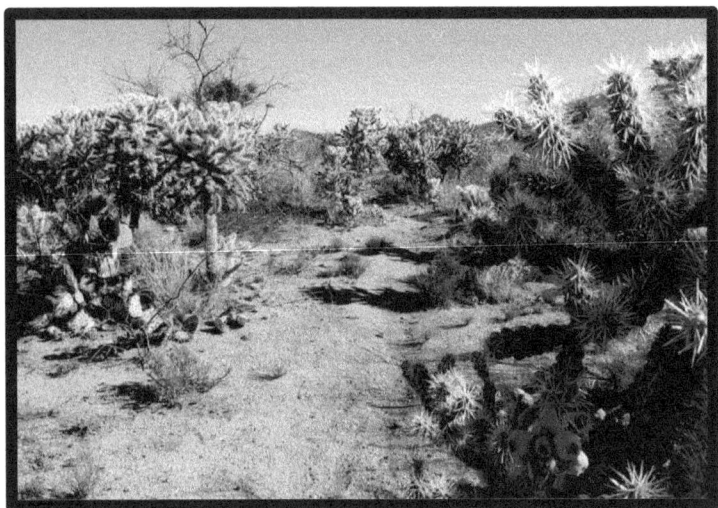

10

Pokey Things

My crumpled Arizona Trail topo map showed the junction to Antelope Tank just up ahead. The tank was a bit off trail and I didn't really need to get extra water as I had enough to make it the rest of the day and hopefully through the night. I'd be hitting the Freeman Road trailhead early in the morning, and a friend of mine had cached a couple gallon jugs of water there for me. I was pretty tired, though, so I paused briefly at the junction and ate a snack. Just a few more miles and I'd find a place to throw down for the night.

Coming out of my break spot, I was making my way up a slight hill when I spotted him. Coiled ever so perfectly just on the edge of the trail.... the light browns and triangular head of a western diamondback rattlesnake. My illusion of safety had been broken. This was the first rattlesnake I'd seen on the Arizona Trail since I left the Mexican border two weeks prior. I thought maybe I wouldn't see any, which was a foolish thought. And now here the two of us were sharing a small stretch of trail somewhere between Oracle and the Gila River in the middle of nowhere.

It was mid-March and typically rattlesnakes don't come out from their holes until a bit later in the year, but we'd had some unusually warm nights and that's all it takes. Three to four warm nights in a row and rattlesnakes all across the Sonoran desert get some sort of primordial message from the depths of their burrows to come on out and join the party.

The problem with this rattlesnake was that he was on the edge of my two-foot wide path, which was neatly contained within a sea of prickly pear cactus and all other manner of pokey things. There was no going around him. Two options: A) I could turn back, or B) he would have to move. I wasn't going to turn back, so he was going to have to move.

I was standing about six or seven feet back from him, eyeballing his triangular head and the ridges on his rattle that weren't moving. The great thing about rattlesnakes is that they normally give hikers plenty of warning with the shaking of their rattle. The rattle is flexible and that unmistakable noise is the sound of each keratin-filled segment knocking against one another as it's being vigorously shaken. I've always been thankful at how loud the rattle is because I've never had any intention of getting too close to one of those things.

But this one wasn't rattling and it wasn't moving although its eyes were wide open. I extended my trekking pole towards its body. It immediately reared back into striking position. My heart pounded and instinctively I took a step back. He was most definitely alive. But he still wasn't moving. I eyeballed the copious amounts of prickly pear on all sides of the trail. I tried to find a way through, but there was nothing. The snake had to go.

I extended my trekking pole again towards the muscular coil and again he rose into striking position. And again he did not move. Time for new tactics.

I crouched down and gathered up a handful of pebbles. I started tossing them one by one so that they would land about an inch or two in front of him. After I had tossed over a dozen, my friend decided that he'd had enough. He dropped his head and slithered into the garden of cactus. I scurried by his former resting spot and on up the hill. I quickly stowed my headphones, deciding that I needed to be able to hear everything that was going on around me as the day's shadows grew long and the vast Arizona sky started to turn vibrant colors of orange, pink and purple.

I hiked on until it was getting really difficult to see. This had been my *modus operandi* when hiking solo. I always found it funny when I'd run into people on the trail and they'd inevitably ask, "Where are you headed tonight?" Most days on the trail I usually didn't know where I was going to finish the day. I tried to go as far as I could and camp right before it got completely dark. Sometimes I had a destination in mind, but that night I didn't.

I had about 15 minutes of daylight left and had been eyeballing flattish-looking spots just off the trail for their sleep suitability. I had two requirements: A) flat enough, and B) big enough for my tent. That's about it. I came down to a gulley of sorts that contained a dry sandy wash. It looked flat enough and wide enough. I glanced up to see an odd sight. There was a tent some 30 yards up the trail on a perch of sorts. I'd been behind my buddy Double T for most of the afternoon, but immediately recognized it was not his tent.

Seeing a tent on a long trail is not really a surprising thing, but we were early in the Arizona Trail hiking season and in the front of the main pack of thru-hikers. We knew that there weren't many people in front of us. I walked up the hill to the tent and met Max. He told me he was hiking the Grand Enchantment Trail and my eyes immediately lit up! I had hiked the GET three years earlier and was surprised and ecstatic to meet another GET hiker in the flesh (the GET and AZT were one in the same on this section of trail)! I had about five minutes of daylight left so I told Max I was going to go set up my tent in the wash and then come back up to talk about his hike.

Instead of walking back down the trail to the wash, I decided to shortcut my way down from his tentsite. It was a fairly short distance.... maybe 50 feet or so. There were some scraggly looking trees on the edge of the wash and I was looking up at them to figure out a way through. And I wasn't looking at where I was stepping. WHACK!!!! Ouch!!!!! No!!!! Something had just nailed the inside of my left ankle. I jumped back three feet, immediately scanning the ground for the serpent that had just struck me. The adrenaline in my body spiked off the charts. It was almost dark and the shadows on the ground appeared to be hiding slithering serpents in the form of dead tree branches. I looked hard.... no snakes. I looked at my ankle. There was a dead piece of jumping cholla attached to it. &$%*!!!!

Jumping cholla (pronounced "choy-ah") look almost fuzzy from a distance. And that's the best place to view this greeter of the Sonoran desert. Regardless of what some folks will tell you, they don't actually jump onto you. The cactus itself is designed so that it's segmented and these segments readily and easily break off from the main stem of the plant when they come in contact with something. It's an efficient means of transport, thus spreading the cactus around and allowing it to proliferate. I had already seen more than one cow walking around southern Arizona with cholla segments attached to its sides. By the way, what a bad lot in life.... a cow in the desert.

Cholla segments tend to be about six inches long and they are covered in spines on all sides, which makes them extremely difficult to remove. You can't just reach down and grab the thing unless, of course, you want a handful of spines.

Not to worry though as I had purchased a "cholla comb" before starting the hike and now I needed to use it. A "cholla comb" looks exactly like a hair pick. Kind of like the one *Quest Love* from *The Roots* always had tucked into his afro. The cholla comb I had been carrying with me was in the top of my backpack. I took my pack off and dug around for it. I slid the comb's teeth between my ankle and the body of the cholla segment and pulled up.

The spines did not want to release. Were these stupid spines barbed like a fishhook??? I pulled harder and it hurt more and finally the main body of the cholla detached. The problem was that this piece of cholla was dead and the spines were brittle. As a result, six of the one-inch long spines were still protruding from my ankle. &$%*!!!!

I grabbed each of the six spines one by one. The first four reluctantly released as I watched the skin from my ankle extend out, trying to hold onto them. The last two spines were so brittle, they kept breaking as I pulled them. The one-inch spine became a half-inch spine then a quarter-inch spine then an eighth-inch and then nothing. The tips of the last two had broken off under the skin of my ankle. &$%*!!!!

I gingerly walked down towards the dry wash, parted the tree branches and made my way onto the soft sand. If my ankle flexed too much in any one direction, the pain was sharp and it was obvious I definitely had the tips of those two cholla spines lodged in there.

I hastily set up my tent, walked back down the wash to the Arizona Trail and up the hill to Max's tent, ignoring the sting in my left ankle. Those spines were embedded and I'd deal with them later. Max and I talked about the GET. He was only five days into the hike, having just started from Phoenix. He had some incredible terrain in front of him: the green ribbon that is Aravaipa Canyon, the lonely rock formations of the Santa Teresa

Wilderness, the sky islands of the Piñalenos, the vast Gila Wilderness and all of New Mexico.

I wished him well on his hike and walked back down the trail and up the wash to my tent. Time for surgery.

I popped on my headlamp and pulled out the lighter and sewing needle I carried in my backpack. I put the flame to the tip of the sewing needle to sterilize it. I took off my sock to see a number of obvious pinholes where the cholla spines had entered my ankle. It wasn't apparent as to which of the holes were covering the broken-off spines. I used my thumbs to push down the tender skin around either side of the holes until I honed in on the two spots that were hiding the broken-off spines.

I used the sewing needle to fish around for the spines, with no luck. I contemplated using my small Swiss army knife to cut the holes open, but thought better of it. Or maybe I just didn't have the stomach for it. Should I get off the trail and go see a doctor? Not sure of what my next move should be, I decided to sleep on it. The 25 miles of hiking that I had just finished left me weary, and I knew my decision-making skills would improve the following morning. I turned off my headlamp, tucked into my sleeping bag and closed my eyes.

~~~

In an effort to beat the heat of an early season warm spell that had descended upon the Arizona Trail, I had been getting up before first light to get some miles in during the cool pre-dawn hours when everything was calm and quiet. I was hiking by five that morning and I thought I'd take it slow and just see how my ankle felt. The first mile was definitely a bit painful and I babied my left foot and ankle a bit trying my best not to flex it too much. It hurt, but was manageable.

I caught up to Double T by 6 a.m. and told him what had happened. That conversation sat on the backburner as we talked about the water cache up ahead at Freeman Road trailhead. Our friend had told us that she was going to put two gallons of water there with our names on it.

We cruised across the gravel parking lot to where a large Arizona Trail sign prominently stood. Behind the sign, nestled in some scrubby mesquite bushes, was a brown metal box. This box was where people cached water for hikers and, sure enough, the two gallons of water with our names on it were in there! We each downed a liter on the spot, then packed out the remaining water for the day's hike. It would be quite dry through this next stretch except for few out-of-the-way windmills and stock tanks.

My ankle had been nagging me again and, at our first break spot, I ducked into the shade on the lee side of a large boulder and pulled out my sewing needle. It was obvious now in the daylight where the spines were embedded. I fished around again and couldn't pry them out. What to do?

Double T told me he was hoping to get to the Gila River bridge by the end of the day. That would be a 30-mile day for him and a 32-mile day for me. And that would be my biggest day yet. Not sure if my ankle would make it that far, I told him that I wasn't certain how far I'd get. I figured that shooting for the Gila River bridge would be a good test of my unsure situation. If my ankle was not happy, I could hitch out to the nearby town of Kearny from the bridge and then get myself to a doctor.

I popped 800 mg of ibuprofen and hit the trail. The rest of the day wasn't nearly as up and down or as steep as the daily miles I had just done between the Mexican border and Oracle. I was happy to have an easier stretch of terrain on which to test my ankle. We'd been intersecting with a number of power line roads and I could see traffic off on a distant highway. Sure enough, I had cell phone service and immediately texted P.O.D.

"Can you look up recommendations on removing cholla spines?" I texted. She hit me back five minutes later with some advice from the web.

"Web says to leave them in if it's not uncomfortable. Use a sterilized needle to get them out if they are bothering you. Duct tape is another option for removing any stragglers from the surface. Try Neosporin on the wound, covered with a Band-Aid to soften the wound and make it easier for digging out with a needle."

Her text gave me hope that I wouldn't need to get off the trail to see a doctor just yet. I immediately threw down my pack, took off my shoe, pulled down my sock, applied some Neosporin and covered my inside anklebone with a beefy Band-Aid.

The rest of the day's hike was hot, but doable, as I headed up and over the sun-baked Tortilla Mountains. I was treated with a rare Gila monster sighting on the backside of the climb. Gila monsters are, in fact, not monsters.... they are slow-moving lizards native to southern Arizona and northern Mexico. And they get quite big. The bigger ones can grow up to two feet in length! They are also the only venomous lizard native to the United States. They spend the bulk of their time underground, so seeing one is a real stroke of luck. I snapped a photo before it scurried away into the depths of the Tortilla Mountains.

My ankle was holding up fairly well and I picked up the pace a bit, trying to get to the Gila River bridge before it was completely dark. I didn't quite make it and had to do the last two miles with the aid of my headlamp.

I popped out onto the paved bridge to see the last hints of daylight towards the west over the Gila River. Incredible. I looked back across the bridge to see the light of a headlamp coming towards me. Double T! He had just come from the water faucet that pokes through the fencing on the side of the local county maintenance building just up the road.

"I'm going to walk up the trail for five or ten minutes and find a spot to throw down," Double T said as he cruised by. "Sounds good. I'll catch you in a few," I replied, heading up the road to that water faucet. It was completely dark by now, but the fence around the county building was easy to spot. I sidled up alongside it and walked its length until reaching the standpipe, which was on the inside of the fence. Only the faucet itself was poking through to allow hikers to access it from the outside of the fence.

When I had hiked the GET a few years prior, this faucet didn't exist. We had to walk up the road a half-mile to get to a trailer park where a "friend of the trail" allowed hikers to get water from his garden hose. I was thankful not to have to walk all the way up to that guy's trailer after having just walked 32 miles.

Why not get water directly from the Gila River, you ask? The Gila is murky, silty and the fast current continually churns up all manner of dirt making it difficult to filter. The faucet on the side of the county maintenance yard was much, much better!

I crouched down and filled up an empty 20-ounce bottle to which I had added some electrolyte mix. I downed the delicious concoction in one bang. Then I stuck my head under the faucet and proceeded to yelp as cold water engulfed my head and face. Words aren't capable of describing how good that cold water felt after 32 miles of heat, dirt and pain.

Refreshed and loaded up with cold clean water, I headed back down the road and up the trail to find Double T camped off to the side in some bushes. I set up my tent and cooked a late dinner. We were both beat and maybe stayed awake another 30 minutes, at the most. The last thing I did before going to sleep was to try once again to fish out the spines. The Neosporin had definitely softened the skin around the spines, but neither tweezers nor the sewing needle were able to extricate the offenders.

The good news was that I was able to hike 32 miles with embedded spines and not experience too much pain. This gave me hope that I'd be able to finish my hike without having to detour to see a doctor.

The ankle hurt less and less each day as I walked north. I passed through the towns of Superior, Pine, and Mormon Lake as I made my way to Flagstaff. I was out of time when I reached Flagstaff as I had only the month of March to hike as far north as I could get. I still had 200 miles of the Arizona Trail left to get to Utah, but that would have to wait for another day.

~~~

Once back in Colorado I made an appointment to see a doctor. The ankle no longer hurt, but those spines were still in there and they needed to come out.

I explained the situation to the doctor who is also a friend of mine. She gave me a shot to numb the ankle and then pulled out a tray of utensils for the extraction. I'm not necessarily a squeamish person but, after eyeballing the scalpel on the tray, I decided it would be best not to watch the procedure too closely. I made small talk with her assistant as she cut open the skin above the spines.

The inside of an anklebone is a difficult place to be impaled. There's not much flesh below the skin. Just skin and bone. And the thing about the tips of cholla spines is that they are covered in microbarbs that help them continue to work their way down into the body. It had been almost a month to the day that I'd had my run in with the dead piece of jumping cholla and, after weeks of hiking long days, these spines had definitely worked their way down into my ankle.

After a few minutes she produced spine tip number one. It was very unmagnificent. Just about 1/8th inch long and woody. I was glad to have it out, but there was still another one down there. She searched around for another five minutes, but was unable to locate it. I can't tell you how thankful I am that we have chemicals that can make a body part go completely numb while a medical professional pokes under skin with metal instruments!

The second spine was left behind. It was likely smaller and encapsulated in scar tissue at this point. She told me that if it continued to give me trouble she could refer me to a specialist that could cut my ankle open all the way to the bone. "I hope I won't have to take you up on that offer," I said, as I shuddered a bit at the thought.

Then she proceeded to stitch me up. Actually it was just one stitch. I've had stitches before for various accidents: cut my head open after running into the side of a cabinet while horse-playing as a preschooler, cut my eyebrow open after running into a basketball post while trying to grab an errant basketball, and a few other minor mishaps here and there. Those were all multiple-stitch affairs. I'd never heard of getting one stitch, but that's all the incision on my ankle called for. So one stitch it was.

The numbing agent wore off and my ankle hurt like hell for a few days. It took a few weeks for things to mend properly, and finally I had the single stitch removed. My ankle healed up, albeit with some scarring to permanently tattoo the spot of the incision. My ankle doesn't bother me anymore, but there's still a little bump there. It's a permanent souvenir from the year I hiked the Arizona Trail, I suppose.... and a constant reminder to look where I'm stepping when in cactus country.

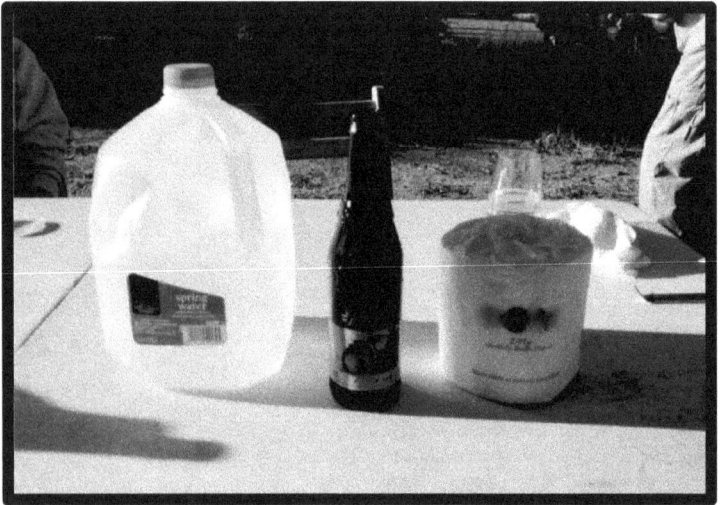

11

Jerry and the Trail Magic Trifecta

S kittles and I had packages to pick up. We walked across US Highway 60 and a dusty parking lot to an adobe building housing Pie Town, New Mexico's tiny post office. We were on the home stretch of our 2006 southbound Continental Divide Trail thru-hike. This would be one of our last mail stops before the final push to the Mexican border.

We gave the postal clerk our ID's and told her we had "general delivery" boxes to pick up. Most people don't know that you can mail yourself a package "general delivery" to almost any and every post office in the United States and the post office is required to hold said package for at least 30 days.

She slid our packages across the countertop and asked how we had been enjoying the trail. "How did you know we were hiking the CDT?" I replied with a laugh. I was wearing all my hiking clothes and had my backpack on. She laughed and said, "You all should check out the VLA if you've got some time."

"The VL who?" I asked.

"The Very Large Array," she replied. She went on to explain that the VLA was the huge satellite dish farm just outside of town featured in the 1997 movie "Contact" starring Jodi Foster. I immediately remembered the movie and had a faint recollection of the satellite dish farm featured in the film.

The VLA is comprised of 27 huge satellite dishes (radio telescopes) arranged in a Y shape. Each dish is over 80 feet in diameter. The complex is run by the National Radio Astronomy Observatory and has been used to further our understanding of black holes, young stars, the Milky Way and a whole host of other astronomical phenomena that are way above my pay grade. It's an incredible sight to behold and one that I would not see during my visit to Pie Town as the VLA was 40 miles away and we were without wheels.

We thanked the postal clerk and walked outside with our boxes. We had only taken about ten steps across the parking lot when two men got out of a car and started walking toward us. "Are you Skittles?" the man with the salt and pepper hair asked. Skittles looked at me, surprised, and then looked back at the man and hesitantly said, "Yeah, I'm Skittles."

The man pulled out a few copies of the *American Profile* magazine article that had featured Skittles and his hike along the Continental Divide. Immediately Skittles was put at ease as he was now certain he wasn't being served a warrant.

We met Skittles on Day 1 of our Continental Divide Trail thru-hike and had kept a similar pace so we got to hike with him a good bit and know him fairly well. Towards the end of our first month out there, a reporter from *American Profile* had come out to Montana to do a story on Skittles and his CDT hike. We weren't there during the actual interview or photo shoot, but thought it was really cool that a fellow long-distance hiker was being featured in a national publication. I had remembered *American Profile* from finding it inserted into the Sunday newspapers my mom used to get when I was a kid. I hadn't thought much of it since then.

The two men who had summoned Skittles in the parking lot were Jerry and Bill from Socorro. Jerry had seen the article on Skittles and shared it with his friend Bill who had hiked most of the CDT through New Mexico. Jerry took us all to breakfast and relayed to Skittles that he had been keeping up with his online trail journal and had a good idea that he was in Pie Town.

At one point during breakfast Bill got up to use the bathroom, and Jerry explained to us that Bill had an inoperable brain tumor in his brain stem. He had brought Bill out here to meet Skittles and some other thru-hikers to help give him hope for recovery and to be able to get back out on the CDT soon. We were moved. Jerry was being an incredible friend to his buddy and we were grateful to be a part of it.

After breakfast we relayed to Jerry that our friend "Speedo" was a half-day or so behind us. We told him he was likely out walking the dirt road into town that very moment. Jerry said to pile in and we'd go find him.

We drove out County Road 603 for about ten miles and spotted a fast moving hiker with a red backpack, capri pants and an orange camo hat. That was Speedo. Jerry and Bill were riding up front and P.O.D., Skittles and I were riding in the back. We told Jerry to keep the tinted back window rolled up so that Speedo couldn't see us and to ask him what the heck he was doing out walking on the road. Jerry slowed his SUV down to a stop and rolled down the window as we crouched down in the back seat.

"What the heck are you doing out here walking the road," Jerry asked Speedo in a funny country accent.

"I'm hiking the Continental Divide Trail," Speedo replied with a big grin on his face. I rolled down the back window and we all started laughing at Speedo. Jerry handed him a slice of pie he had nabbed from one of the pie shops back in Pie Town (of course there are pie shops in Pie Town).

~ ~ ~

On November 6th our group finally made it to the Mexican border down near the Crazy Cook Monument in New Mexico's boothill. We completely lucked out by catching a 20+ mile ride back to the partially abandoned town of Hachita from a U.S. Border Patrol agent.

Incidentally, if you are looking to disappear, on the lam or need to lay low for a while, I'd recommend checking out real estate around Hachita, New Mexico.

The border patrol agent dropped us in front of one of Hachita's abandoned buildings where a friend of ours was waiting to shuttle us to Deming, the closest large town with a hotel. We all piled into a room at Motel 6. It was late and we were whipped from hiking all day and into the night to finish the trail. Exhausted and spent, we all passed out.

Before retiring, Skittles had gotten word that Jerry and Bill were planning to drive down to Deming to celebrate the finish with us. We joined them at breakfast the following morning. I had the prickly pear omelet. It was delicious.

P.O.D., myself and our friend "No Trace" ended up taking a ride with Jerry and Bill back to Socorro. We overnighted at Jerry's place and got to meet Anyssa, his partner in crime. Jerry graciously drove us all to the Albuquerque airport the next morning to rent a car for our drive back to Colorado. We were blown away by Jerry's willingness to help us out. From the breakfast in Pie Town, to meeting up with us in Deming, to the ride back to Socorro, and now a quick trip to Albuquerque, Jerry had become a "trail angel" without even knowing it.

~~~

The following summer I got an email from Skittles. Jerry had reached out to let him know that Bill had passed. They were planning a ceremony for Bill and were hoping some of us had pictures of him. Bill had hiked all of the CDT from Mexico to the town of Cuba in northern New Mexico. Bill's friends and family were planning to spread his ashes somewhere along the Gila River, one of the most scenic sections of the trail in all of New Mexico.

~~~

Fast forward to 2014 ... Skittles and I decided to head back out to the Southwest for some hiking. The Grand Enchantment Trail runs 800 miles from Phoenix to Albuquerque through some of the most desolate and spellbinding landscape you can imagine. Skittles was biding time until he started a seasonal job and I wouldn't be busy with forestry work here in Colorado until the snow melted, so we had the perfect window to hike the GET in March and April.

800 miles is a short distance when compared with the 2,600+ miles we had hiked on the CDT in 2006, but those 800 miles pack a punch. By the time we had crossed from Arizona into New Mexico, we were feeling a bit worse for wear. P.O.D. came out to join us for our first week in New Mexico's Gila Wilderness for what turned out to be our toughest week on the entire GET. After P.O.D. left we had two weeks to go until finishing the trail at the base of Albuquerque's Sandia Mountains.

Skittles had kept in touch with Jerry over the past eight years and had mentioned that Jerry and Anyssa wanted to meet up with us. Mentioning Jerry's name brought back a flood of fond memories from the end of our CDT hike in 2006. It also made me think of Bill and feel gratitude for being healthy and able to live out my dream hiking long trails.

Turns out that our next town stop in Magdalena was less than a 30 minute drive from Jerry's place in Socorro. Magdalena is a small ranching community west of Socorro and, oddly enough, only 25 miles from the VLA! However, we wouldn't get a shot at the VLA this go around either. But we would get a shot at reuniting with Jerry and Anyssa after eight years. Skittles gave Jerry a ballpark idea of when we'd get to Magdalena and, like clockwork, we walked into town about 30 minutes before Skittles' projected arrival time. It's amazing to me how accurate hikers are when predicting when they'll get to towns (especially towns that have restaurant food).

Apparently Magdalena, New Mexico, is not a good place to show up on a Sunday. We briefly scouted the small downtown to find nothing was open. Thoughts of going out to lunch with Jerry and Anyssa were dashed. We wandered over to the public library (also closed) to loiter a bit. Even the standpipe outside the main building of the public library had a pad lock on it. No water to be found here either, but at least there was shade from the sun on the deck behind the library.

We would later learn from a friend who had hiked the GET the year before that there was NO WATER in Magdalena. He had checked into a local motel, gotten his room key and started to walk to his room when the motel clerk handed him a couple of water bottles and briefly mentioned that the town's water supply had gone dry and there wasn't any running water. None. And that meant the shower he had been dreaming about taking for the last few days would have to wait for another day. To add insult to injury, later that evening he found himself precariously scooping up two scorpions slowly moving about under his bed, which he swiftly escorted back outside. Apparently there was no extra charge for the bottled water or the scorpions.

Jerry and Anyssa must have known about the parched situation in Magdalena because they showed up with a cooler filled to the brim with beer, soda, Gatorade and water!! I couldn't decide which to drink first so I had one of each.

"Doesn't look like much is open for lunch," I dejectedly said to Jerry and Anyssa.

"Not a problem at all," Jerry said with a smile on his face. He and Anyssa pulled out another cooler from their vehicle. He opened the lid and whipped out fried chicken, ribs, grilled chicken, coleslaw, noodle salad, carne asada and a bunch of chips and other picnic fixings.

"Holy Moly!" I exclaimed, looking at all the food that had magically appeared on the deck behind the library. "This is incredible," I said, thanking them profusely as I filled my plate to maximum capacity. Skittles and I were close to the 600-mile mark of our hike and our appetites had grown to a ridiculous size. I had three platefuls before I called it good. I could have eaten more, but doing so would have put me at risk of not being able to hike out and we still had miles to make before the day was done.

The Grand Enchantment Trail had been a mostly a solitary experience for Skittles and me. This was one of our first and only opportunities to share the hike with other people. We all sat on the porch, enjoying great food and getting caught up on the last eight years. It was a lot of fun and we were reluctant to leave, but alas, leaving is what long distance hikers do time and time again. Jerry had inquired about our route heading north from Magdalena to Albuquerque. Skittles showed him his map and he spied the trail's crossing under I-25.

"Hey, this spot is fairly close to where we live. When do you think you'll get there?" Jerry asked. Skittles and I did some quick math and determined we'd likely be there around 6 p.m. the following evening. "We'll meet you there," Jerry said with a smile on his face.

We thanked Jerry and Anyssa for coming out to rescue us and we hiked out of town. I wasn't moving that swiftly after three plates of food and four beverages. I was quite happy though. I had a stupid grin all the way to the patch of junipers seven or so miles from town where we hunkered down for the night. Our time in Magdalena would have been a bit grim without Jerry and Anyssa, and we were lucky they came out to see us.

The wind that plagued us most of that evening finally died out by the first hint of dawn. We were both brimming with energy from the previous day's calorie boost in Magdalena. We made quick work of the morning's hike, although the noonday sun was starting to shine bright and hot.

Just as the sun was starting to drain our energy levels and motivation, we popped into San Lorenzo Canyon to find a little bit of Utah there in New Mexico. The rock walls allowed us to sit in the shade to enjoy the ice-cold spring water we had just filled our water bottles with. We hiked out of that break reinvigorated and looking forward to our rendezvous with Jerry and Anyssa.

The narrow confines of San Lorenzo Canyon soon dissipated as we passed the last of its robust cottonwood trees. The canyon opened up into a dry sandy wash that was 50 feet wide, bordered by wide sagebrush flats. We continued east heading slightly downhill toward the Rio Grande. The afternoon shadows had become long when I spotted I-25 off in the distance.

As we got closer to the interstate I could see that we'd go right under the road and the speeding cars oblivious to our pilgrimage. We followed remnant tire treads in the sand as we walked under the highway. The dark and dingy underpass looked like a scene straight out of *Breaking Bad*. I half expected one *Mike Ehrmantraut* to be standing there in the shadows, ready to hand off a bag of money.

As soon as we popped out on the east side of I-25, we crossed a set of train tracks and came up to one of the series of canals that divert water from the Rio for agriculture. A dirt road paralleled the canal and, sure enough, we spotted Jerry and Anyssa's vehicle. It was 6 o'clock on the dot and once again we had arrived on time. Jerry and Anyssa were busy setting up a folding picnic table with chairs. This was too much. In my 15,000 miles of long distance hiking, I had never had anyone set up a dinner table with chairs trailside to feed me and a buddy.

Upon the table for us was a six pack of cold beer, two gallons of water, two rolls of toilet paper and the best green chile chicken enchiladas (with a fried egg on top) that I have ever had in my life. I was speechless. And then I laughed at the toilet paper. Beer, water, toilet paper.... the trail magic trifecta!

Skittles and I threw our packs down, pulled out a chair, gave thanks and praise to Jerry and Anyssa, and commenced to eat every bite of enchiladas and down every ounce of beer present before us. We packed out the toilet paper for later, of course.

As we hiked out from the canal, I admired the irony of it all. Here Skittles and I were two dirty vagabonds walking across New Mexico's sandy washes and open spaces, just 30 minutes prior, being treated to an incredible trailside dinner by two incredible people we had the pleasure of calling friends. How lucky we were. How lucky we are.

12

Romantish

They say your actions in the face of adversity are a mirror of who you are. They say that from the comfort of a climate-controlled home, showers with hot water, clean clothes, and beer in the fridge, with not the least bit of adversity to consider. I say it's much easier to be your best self when not faced with adversity and to remember and learn from previous mistakes when you are.

Our first hike together was 145 days long. I can't really recommend a 145 day hike as a good starting point for a new relationship or a way to increase the chances that the relationship will last, but that's what we did. We hiked 145 days side by side, sometimes in silence, sometimes happy as clams, and sometimes wondering what the hell we had gotten ourselves into.

In the normal world most couples don't spend every minute of every day together. You go to work and are apart for eight or more hours. You see each other in the evenings for a few hours and then you go to bed. You might end up actually spending about three to five hours a day with your significant other. On trail you spend every minute of every day with that person. You see every single side of your darling: the good, the bad, the ugly and much much more. You see them at their best and at their worst. You learn their weaknesses and strengths. And most of this you learn within the first month of hiking with them.

P.O.D. and I did have the benefit of being long-distance hikers before we met each other, but neither of us had ever hiked with someone else as a "thru-couple." Perhaps that's why we didn't think twice about jumping in feet first. That, and we were both pretty young at the time. Had we known what we knew at the end of those 145 days walking from Canada to Mexico along the Continental Divide Trail, we may have hired a therapist to do the entire hike with us.

The trials and tribulations came early on our CDT hike. We were not mentally or physically prepared for all that Montana would throw at us. Set aside the fact that neither one of us had previous experience learning to compromise as hiker couples must do to stay on trail and intact. The first six weeks on the CDT were unbelievably demanding.

The year we hiked the CDT was unusually hot and buggy. It was the third hottest summer on record in Montana (at least until the year we hiked it - 2006). Trying to be a decent person and a loving partner is astonishingly difficult when you are dealing with a mosquito horde in the hot sun, as well as trying to figure out which steep hill you are supposed to climb on the other side of the boggy meadow in which you are now standing ankle deep in muddy brown water. Really, really difficult.

I'll admit that patience has never been my strong suit. I've become better at it over the years, but I had to learn a lot about finding that zen state when in the midst of adversity. I've still got a lot to learn. I definitely knew a lot less as a 30-year-old on a CDT thru-hike with my new girlfriend. I hit multiple breaking points on the trail that year, the first of which took place at Dana Spring.

I suppose that during the right time of year (perhaps a crisp autumn day) Dana Spring is a nice place to spend an afternoon. There's a water source there and a patch of trees to take a nice rest break. There's the wide open Montana skies to gaze at. Heck, you could probably pack in the makings for a nice picnic lunch and have a truly memorable afternoon there.

The day P.O.D. and I got to Dana Spring was a complete disaster. I had been writing a page a night in a journal while on the CDT, and my journal entry from that day contained one sentence: "Today was the worst day I've ever had on a long trail." The day that was Dana Spring was actually a culmination of all the adversity that we had faced during those first three weeks of the hike.

P.O.D. had been dealing with a lingering groin injury and a more recent strain to one of her quads. She hobbled around as best she could those first three weeks, but her pace was slow. The 50,000+ feet of elevation gain that the CDT threw at us through Glacier National Park, the

Bob Marshall and Scapegoat Wilderness Areas, and the section between the towns of Lincoln and MacDonald Pass did not help, either.

We had fallen into this rhythm of my gradually hiking ahead as long as the trail was obvious, and then I'd stop and wait for her to catch up. The day we hiked into Dana Spring was no different. I came down the hill to spy a cement trough in the middle of an unshaded clearing. I'd had my mosquito head net on all day, not to keep mosquitos away, but to keep the deer flies and horse flies that were circling my dome from biting me. I don't know what it was about that cement trough but, when I stopped beside it to fill up my water bottles, the bugs were in a manic frenzy.

I filled up my bottles as quickly as possible and retreated to a small stand of fir trees on the edge of the clearing. The bugs were slightly less frantic in the trees but bad enough that I realized rather quickly that this rest break was going to be anything but restful unless I found shelter.

I've been forced to set up my tent only a handful of times in the middle of the day just to get away from bugs, but this day was one of them. I pulled our tent from my backpack and set it up in record time. I dove in and, even though it was touching 90 degrees in the sun, it felt just as warm in the tent but at least I was bug free.

I had a slightly obscured view of Dana Spring from the screen door of the tent, thanks to the waterfall of branches from the fir tree I was tucked under. I checked frequently to see if P.O.D. was coming down the hill. I pulled out my snack bag to see if there was anything interesting to munch on. The heat had killed my appetite and nothing looked enticing. I looked out the tent again toward Dana Spring. All I could see was a crumpled P.O.D. sitting on the ground about ten feet from the cement trough, crying.

I jumped out of the tent, put my mosquito head net and jacket on and hustled over to where she sat in the dirt. "What's going on?" I asked, flummoxed. She was too choked up to answer and I had been too busy digging around in my food bag to see her trip and fall. The flies were reaching a frenzied pitch once again and I told her I had the tent set up in the trees and she should come over and get in.

P.O.D. slowly got up and was limping worse than I'd seen her limp on any day of the hike thus far. We both climbed in the tent and I quickly smashed the few deer flies that had flown in with us. P.O.D. still hadn't said a word. She lay down and started sobbing. This was truly a miserable situation. It was 90 degrees, we were filthy, there was an army of biting flies outside our tent just waiting to drain blood, the tent felt like a sauna and there was nowhere to go. I could think of a thousand places I'd rather be. And P.O.D. was lying beside me, sobbing without saying a word. I lasted another two minutes and then blurted out, "If this is how it's going to be the rest of the summer, I'm quitting the trail. I can't take this. This is miserable. Why are you crying?"

I was exasperated. There was a long silence and then P.O.D. finally explained to me that her groin had really been killing her all morning and that she just wanted to get to Dana Spring. And 15 feet before the trough she tripped, fell, bloodied her knee and hurt her groin again. "What? When did that happen?" I asked, confused.

"Just now," she said.

She showed me the gash on her knee, which looked rough. We spent the rest of our "break" in almost total silence, feeling as if the hike were doomed. It just didn't seem feasible to continue on with her injuries, coupled with the heat and bugs as ruthless as they were. I had already been making other summer plans in my head because I didn't feel we'd be out on the CDT much longer.

Somehow we managed 22 miles that day and 14 miles to the road into Helena the next day. We took almost 3 days off in Helena to let P.O.D.'s injuries mend a bit. We got back on the trail loaded up with bug spray and a stronger resolve to make the hike tolerable. I even got some all-mesh bug pants that made me look like Amanda Bellows in *I Dream of Jeannie*. I'd wear them in the late afternoons when the bugs would start to multiply. They looked absolutely ridiculous and yet they absolutely kept me sane through the rest of bug season.

Over time P.O.D.'s groin and quad injuries got better. They never fully resolved themselves, but they got to a manageable stasis, especially once we got out of Montana and onto flatter terrain in Wyoming and the well-graded trails of Colorado. We had both assumed that all of the CDT would be as tough as Montana and we were ready to throw in the towel. Had we done so we would have never known the trail did, in fact, get a bit easier. And we likely would have parted ways, deeming our hike and our hiking partnership a failure. In reality, all we needed was a few days off.

~~~

There was also the matter of maps. I've been reading maps since I was a fifteen-year-old in an Outward Bound course. As a working Forester, I read and navigate with maps almost every day I'm on the job. I'm a lot more comfortable with maps and navigation than most. It's not because I'm naturally good at it, it's just that I've done it often enough that it's become second nature.

We were still trying to suss out the business of hiking as a couple after we left Helena. One thing I had taken upon myself to be in charge of was navigating once the trail disappeared and we became "misplaced." I say misplaced because the word "lost" is somewhat inaccurate. To be truly lost means you have no clue where you are. This was never the case on the CDT. We'd be hiking along on a trail and then all of a sudden there was no trail. A lot of times in Montana I would be out in front as P.O.D. was hobbling along more slowly with a bum leg. The trail would disappear and I'd stop, pull out the map, turn the GPS unit on, determine my current location, figure out where the trail should be, figure out where the trail was supposed to go, spot the general location up ahead and continue hiking. P.O.D. would catch me and I'd tell her I was "pretty sure" we needed to head such and such direction and I'd start walking.

P.O.D. did what most hikers do when they are unsure of whether or not they are hiking in the right direction. She slowed down to half the speed she normally hiked, while looking around and simultaneously trying to read the guidebook. We had decided during the first week on the trail that she would carry the guidebook and I'd carry the maps and GPS unit. I'd end up getting frustrated that she was walking so slowly and we'd get into an argument. Then we'd spend a few hours walking along in silence, mad at each other. Rinse and repeat.

It took us over a month to finally figure out that we both needed maps. We only had one map set so Plan B was that we needed to be together to make navigational decisions that we both understood and agreed with. After all, we were a team. And we also learned that it's much easier to make good navigational decisions in the shade of a tree than out in the heat of a relentless sun.

From then on when the trail disappeared, I'd find a shady spot to stop, turn on the GPS unit and wait for P.O.D. We used the GPS to find our exact location on our map and then we'd both talk over the best way to get from where we were to where we needed to go. We'd both be on the same page; we could go full speed ahead instead of at the half speed of doubt and uncertainty.

We slowly figured out a division of labor that worked for our hike. I'd set up the tent and sleeping bags/pads while P.O.D. cooked our evening meal. We shared a single cookpot and did our best to go spoonful for spoonful so that we both got the same amount of food. I'd clean the cookpot (most of the time) and go tie our bear bag to a tree well away from camp.... a precaution we took rather seriously as the first 1,000 miles of our CDT hike was in grizzly country. P.O.D. found herself taking on the role of team cheerleader. She was less inclined to get rattled by whatever daily disaster came our way. Me, not so much.

~~~

As the miles accumulated, our arguments became less and less and the hike got better and better until we got to the middle of Colorado. 2006 brought three early season snowstorms to Colorado's high country in September. Each storm got progressively worse. The final storm dropped two feet of snow on the Divide. We had gone from a miserably hot hike in Montana to a miserably cold hike in Colorado in a matter of months. It wasn't uncommon for us to end up camping on snow after that final September snowstorm. It was this type of adversity that brought out the worst in us. Our patience would grow thin and we'd be more prone to snap at each other. Things came to a head as we left the town of Creede.

We spent two days postholing in deep snow from Creede, trying to get back up to the Divide. Once we got back to the trail, it immediately disappeared as everything was covered in a sea of white. The going was super slow and we had to stop frequently to figure out where we were and where we were supposed to be going. Given the slow, snowy travel, we had to pack extra food, which made our packs heavier. Winter had come early to Colorado and we had no other choice but to deal with it.

We had overnighted in Pagosa Springs and resupplied for the next stretch of trail from Wolf Creek Pass to Cumbres Pass. We made an executive decision to do a road walk through Platoro Canyon on the east side of the divide instead of hiking the snowbound CDT that spent much of its time above treeline. However, we would have to hike on the CDT initially for a half-day or so out of Wolf Creek Pass before we could bail out to the county roads that traversed Platoro Canyon – a seldom seen and infrequently visited valley in the southernmost reaches of Colorado.

Almost immediately after hiking out of Wolf Creek Pass, we lost the trail in deep snow and slowed down to a crawl. We had been reduced to about a mile per hour, having to check our maps and GPS unit every five to ten minutes just to stay in the general vicinity of where we were supposed to be. We finally got to Railroad Pass and made a wrong decision, which led to a wrong turn. We lost an hour hiking and then backtracking and I began to build mountains out of hills in my mind.

"Was the entire hike to Cumbres Pass going to be like this? I don't have enough food to last all the way, if that's the case," I thought to myself. Black clouds filled my brain as we trudged on. I was pissed at P.O.D. too. She had said some things about a guy we met in Creede that really rubbed me the wrong way. I focused on that and decided this was the perfect time to have an argument about it. The day was wrecked.... mainly because I fed the flames that let it become a wreck.

We finally managed to get back on track and down into Platoro Canyon where the dirt road walking was snow free. Our attitudes improved dramatically. Even so, the months and miles of hiking the CDT and the trials and tribulations of hiking as a couple had worn me down. I desperately wanted a vacation from the vacation. I told P.O.D. that I wanted to take a week off trail by myself. She looked at me blankly. We hiked on.

My finances weren't such that I could splurge for seven nights in a hotel room and what was P.O.D. going to do while I was hiding from her and the trail? We only had about a month left and decided to plod on. Our second day of hiking in New Mexico, we caught our friend Skittles. I think most couples are inclined to put on a "good face" when a new person is in their midst. Skittles may have saved our relationship just by being the third person in our crew.

We put our differences aside and spent the days shooting the breeze with Skittles. By luck a couple of local hunters invited us to overnight at their camp. They fed us bowls of steaming *pozole* and cold beers. After we hiked past Mt. Taylor, the trail descended in elevation permanently and our days of postholing in snow were finally behind us. The trail never got easy, but the hike through New Mexico didn't seem like a constant battle against adversity and each other.

~ ~ ~

One final test of our relationship on the CDT came the day before we finished. We arrived in Hachita, our last trail town in New Mexico, as part of a group of six hikers. It had been fun walking together with this dodgy crew of veteran long-distance hikers. Skittles, Speedo, Pi and No Trace made our run to the border a lot more enjoyable.

We had hiked into the town of Hachita well after dark and were looking for a place to throw down after seeing that both the bar and *tienda* were closed. Not a single one of us saw the "No Camping" sign tacked up near the flat ground surrounding the town's water tower. That's exactly where we set up our tents. Luckily for us, this area was hidden from view by the ten-foot mesquite bushes and tall grasses that covered the area.

We spent the following morning lollygagging at the post office and around town. The postmaster was kind enough to let us fill up our water bottles at her house as the local store was still closed and, for the life of us, we could not find anywhere else in town to get water. It wasn't until noon that we actually started moving south again on the CDT.

We hiked a quick six miles along the road and took a break. Then we hiked another five miles to the junction with State Highway 34. Decision time. Back in 2006, the

CDT still had a lot of unfinished trail and road walking where trail had yet to be constructed. Oddly enough, the CDT had just been signed from the road junction where we were now standing and continued 28 miles to the Mexican border at a distant and lonely place called the Crazy Cook Monument (it was named after the crazy cook that murdered someone at that very spot "in cold blood" with an axe a long, long time ago).

For me it was a no-brainer to take the newly signed and marked CDT the 28 miles from this junction to the finish, but not for the rest of the group. A heated debate ensued. Somebody proposed we walk a random dirt road due east for 10 miles to where it stopped at the border. Someone else mentioned continuing south on the paved road to Antelope Wells where the road crossed into Mexico at a border guard station. Other folks simply didn't care. It was all sort of arbitrary, I supposed, as the actual Continental Divide was well west of us but on private property and inaccessible to hikers.

I don't know why I felt so adamant about doing the signed CDT route to its finish, but I did. Maybe it was because we had spent so much time navigating and wishing the CDT existed in places where it didn't. Maybe it was because we knew there were three water sources along the signed route. Maybe it was because I was exhausted from walking for four and a half months and didn't want to have to navigate and route-find anymore.... I just wanted to follow the signs. It was probably a mix of all that.

I knew that I didn't want to walk the road shoulder of the paved highway to Antelope Wells. And I didn't feel that walking an arbitrary county dirt road 10 miles out to the border was worthy of a proper CDT finish even though Pi offered to pull one of the new CDT signs out of the ground and carry it across his back "like Jesus."

We had been debating at this intersection for almost an hour. Tempers were starting to flare (mine in particular). At some point I got pissed off that there were three other about to be "triple crowners" (people who have hiked the AT, PCT and CDT) in our group, and none of them seemed to care that much about where they were going to finish the triple crown. We'd hit a stalemate and at that point I pulled P.O.D. to the side.

"Do you not give a shit where we finish?" I asked, dumbfounded.

"Not really, but I'm not finishing the triple crown," she said.

"I feel like an ass for making such a big deal out of this. I just don't get it. We've been walking almost five months and we're about to finish. Half of them don't care where we finish and the other half want to walk some random dirt road when we for once have actual marked trail to the border," I said, keyed up and red-faced.

"Yeah, but it's 28 miles to the middle of nowhere and then we'll have to turn around and walk 28 miles back to this road just to hitch back to Hachita. That could take three full days," P.O.D. said, making sure I completely understood what following the CDT route meant.

She had a good point. There wasn't going to be anyone waiting for us at the border, and it would definitely be a drag to get to the finish only to have to retrace our footsteps for 28 miles to get back to the junction with the paved highway.

I continued to make my case to her in private, which is difficult to do on the side of the road with four other hikers sitting nearby.

"Tell me what you want to do because when we finish this hike, I'm going back to Crested Butte with you and not with any of these people," P.O.D. offered as an olive branch and a way to calm me down.

"I want to finish the CDT where the CDT finishes even if it means having to walk another 28 miles to get back out," I stated emphatically. This wasn't ideal and I think I knew that in the back of my head, but my 30-year-old self had backed myself into a corner and I was too bull-headed to waver.

"You realize we might be splitting from the group then?" P.O.D. said, a bit uneasy.

I didn't like the thought of that either. All of us had hiked the last month together and, on the afternoon of the day before we were to finish, our discussion on where to finish had devolved into an argument.

"Yeah, I realize this. If that's what has to happen, it has to happen," I said still not able to see how the other options were better options.

P.O.D. later told me she thought it was a no-win situation and that all the options were bad. She decided to go with what I wanted because she really didn't care where we finished, but she wanted to have my back.

"Backing up your partner on small things can have a big payoff in the long run," she told me months later when we were rehashing the events of that strange day.

When I told the group that P.O.D. and I were going to finish the trail at Crazy Cook, I fully expected that we'd be parting ways with everyone. It seemed like the rest of the crew was leaning towards the 10-mile road walk finish, which made a lot more sense on paper. You could easily hike 10 miles, tag the border, and hike 10 miles back to the highway in a day.

Ultimately, they decided to join P.O.D. and me for the Crazy Cook finish. They didn't want the group to break up.

I felt like a scoundrel all that final day. I hiked by myself for a good portion of it and there was definitely tension in the air.

The three water sources that were supposed to be on the route to Crazy Cook didn't quite pan out. We found the first one, but not the second one. We arrived to the third and final one only to peer into the neck-high water tank to see what looked like the contents of a long-abandoned pool at a closed-down motel. I was really feeling like a bum at this point. I had convinced all these people to come with me to the Crazy Cook Monument to finish. We were out of water and our final water source looked like the remnants of a Superfund site. And we would have to wake up tomorrow and hike 28 miles back to the road. Yeah, I felt like a real bum.

I climbed down from the rusty water tank and heard the engine of a vehicle off in the distance. The sound was getting closer. I hustled out to the nearby dirt road to find a US Border Patrol vehicle pulling up. I walked up to the driver's side and said, "Hey there's six of us finishing the Continental Divide Trail and we're out of water. Do you have any water on you?"

"I don't have any water, but I can give you a ride back to Hachita," he said, matter-of-fact! This was a game changer. And this saved our collective asses from going thirsty and my ass from being the idiot that lead our crew to its demise.

"I've got to go check on a few things, but I can meet you at the monument in an hour," the Border Patrol agent told me.

"Sounds good. We're headed there right now," I said as I turned away to go tell the group the news.

An hour later, just like clockwork, a border patrol vehicle crept right up to the Crazy Cook Monument without its lights on. Our border patrol agent was using his night vision goggles to navigate. We had just finished celebrating and were happy to pile into his vehicle for the ride back to town.

So it ended well, but that was mostly luck. Today, my 40-year-old self wouldn't have been so resolute about finishing at a specific spot in the middle of nowhere that no one else cared about finishing at.

~~~

P.O.D. and I had planned to move in together after the CDT, but thought better of it. It's a fairly permanent decision and we needed a break from each other after 145 days of the toughest hike either of us had ever done. Months passed and things continued to get better and better. We eventually moved in together the following year and P.O.D. began discussing a thru-hike of the Pacific Crest Trail. She asked me to stay home and take care of her dog while she was out hiking.

This was difficult. I had hiked the PCT in 2004 and it had been my favorite long hike to date. I loved almost everything about my time out there. I even loved the first 700 miles from the Mexican Border to the Sierra, which most hikers loathe due to the hot temperatures and big water carries. I loved the fact that it didn't rain a single day for the first four months I was out there. I loved the gradual graded climbs and descents. I loved the volcanic terrain in Oregon and Washington. I loved the diversity of ecosystems through which the trail wandered. And I knew how much P.O.D. was going to love it and how much I'd go crazy knowing she was out there and I wasn't. Stay home and take care of the dog. Yeah, right.

After a week or so I told P.O.D. all the things I just told you about the PCT and more. I told her that I wanted to join her. I told her that if we were not capable or comfortable hiking together, then we shouldn't be together. And I told her there was no possible way on God's green earth that I could stay at home for five months working a mindless job and taking care of her dog while she was out hiking the most fantastic long-distance trail in the United States.

She explained her apprehension to hike another long trail together after all that had happened on the CDT. It made sense and I understood her reluctance. The PCT wasn't the CDT, though, and I made the case that we'd face a lot less adversity on the PCT and, as a result, the hike would be a lot different and a lot more enjoyable.

And it was. Except for the 10 days we hiked through the Sierra way too early in the season with no resupply. That was our fault, though. We knew better and hiked in about two weeks too early anyway at our own peril.

The morning we finally popped out of the Sierra into the little outpost at Red's Meadow was to be our salvation. We had spent over a week hiking from Trail Pass without going out for resupply. We had only briefly seen a small handful of other thru-hikers as it was still the first week of June. We'd crossed way too many raging creeks running way too fast and strong with snowmelt. We had gone up and over seven high passes including 13,200' Forester Pass, the PCT's highest point. We were weary, dirty and had grown so tired of the sad salty noodles we ate every night that we decided to skip dinner the last night before Red's Meadow. We knew there was a restaurant there and decided we'd tough it out until morning and then eat one of the biggest breakfasts in the history of the trail!

We were up early and a bit giddy; we were finally going to get a taste of civilization after many days of hardship and high mountain passes. I wanted an omelet and hash browns. And toast and coffee. And maybe a second omelet and hash browns. I wasn't exactly sure. I wanted it all.

Red's Meadow was closed. We got there too early in June. They had not yet opened for the season. I sat down in the dirt and put my head in my hands. I was as deflated as a decrepit mylar balloon stuck in a tree from a long ago birthday party. I laid back in the dirt and stared up at the sky. I had no words.

P.O.D. was wandering around the scattering of buildings that comprise civilization at Red's Meadow. The café was most definitely closed, but she heard voices coming from the back of the building. She walked around. The voices were in Spanish and it just so happens that P.O.D. is fluent in Spanish.

parRomantish

Five minutes later P.O.D. opened the front door of the café from the inside and motioned for me to come in. There were four folks in the café getting it ready to open for the season.... the following week! They made both of us a plate of food on the spot!! The plate included bacon and at that time in my life I didn't eat swine. That morning I ate bacon with a grin on my face. I couldn't believe our luck. And then I realized it wasn't luck, it was P.O.D. If it had been just me.... this gringo would have just kept walking and probably never had the opportunity to meet the folks in the café. P.O.D. got to know all of them quite well in the short time we were there. They turned down our offer of money to cover the meals. They wished us well and we thanked them profusely as we walked out the door with full stomachs.

~~~

Our 2,000 mile hike of New Zealand's long trail, Te Araroa (pronounced Tay Air-uh-RO-uh), found us facing other conundrums. The TA is much more of an urban hike rather than a wilderness hike like you'd find on the Pacific Crest and Continental Divide Trails here in the States. We had heard great things about the TA from a trusted friend of ours and had high expectations about hiking it. Our friend lied. And we no longer trust him. That's not entirely true, but it is.

So early into our four-month hike of the TA, we realized that what we had signed up for was not the bill of goods that we had bought. Given that we had sold our house in Colorado, quit our jobs, put everything in storage and

241

flown 9,000 miles to the other side of the planet to hike this trail, we couldn't simply quit the hike because it wasn't what we'd hoped for.

Instead of having to suck it up and adjust our schedule for three weeks like we did back when hiking the GR11 in Spain, we had three and half more months left to be in New Zealand. P.O.D. was really angry. She had left a job she loved and in which she felt her work made a real difference to do this hike. I wasn't as angry as I didn't have as much at stake. I was more-or-less taking a break from my job as a forestry consultant of which I was my company's only employee. My "boss" had given me the time off and I knew when I got back home, I'd be able to start up work again where I had left off. P.O.D. would be searching for an entirely new job.

We leaned hard on our experience adjusting our expectations in Spain and the lessons we had learned while dealing with adversity on the CDT. Luckily the TA wasn't exceptionally difficult; it was just boring, and it had way too much road walking.

New Zealand is comprised of two large islands. While hiking the North Island we kept being told, "Wait till you get to the South Island.... it's much better down there." The South Island contained the second longest road walk (135 miles) on the entire TA and avoided many of the scenic wonders that have made New Zealand famous. Sure it was slightly better than the North Island, but by no means did it salvage the hike.

Accept, Adapt, and Appreciate is what our friend Swami says. We recognized that this wasn't going to be the four-month hike we thought it would be and did our best to accept this reality. Then we adapted as best we could. And finally we came to appreciate the people of New Zealand who are the true gem of a TA hike. You'll never meet friendlier people on this planet. I'd be friendlier, too, knowing I'd never have to go bankrupt trying to pay for health care, but that's a story for another day.

~~~

The other thing about New Zealand - a tragedy narrowly averted - occurred while we were hiking with Skittles. Every hiker has a different pace. It's not uncommon that I'll take off on the uphills and get a bit ahead of P.O.D. She and I have relatively the same pace on flats and downhills. Typically, I'll lead the way on a climb and then hang out on top for P.O.D.

We had been walking a short stretch of beach before a section that led up into some bluffs. The day was overcast and drizzly. I took off and spent thirty minutes making the climb to the top. It was a bit windy, drizzly and foggy up top so, instead of stopping, I kept moving. I knew Skittles was behind, hiking up with P.O.D., so I didn't hesitate in moving on. We usually had a snack break every couple of hours and I figured that they would catch me at some point.

After another thirty minutes passed, I got the urge to offload some previously consumed food. I ducked off the trail into the jungle and took care of business. All told I was probably off trail just shy of ten minutes. I resumed hiking and noticed a new set of footprints had appeared heading in the same direction. Long-distance hikers get pretty good at identifying who is on trail by the footprints of their shoe treads and I immediately recognized the new footprints as P.O.D.'s. She had scooted past me while I was off digging a hole.

I picked up the pace to try and catch her. 10 minutes went by. Then 20. Then 30. She was hauling ass! I picked up the pace even more and started speed-walking. Finally after 45 minutes, I rounded a bend in the trail and could just make out the back of her backpack.

"HEY YOU, QUIT HIKING SO FAST!" I yelled.

P.O.D. turned around confused. I ran up to her. "I thought you were in front of me," she said a bit out of breath.

"Yeah, I could tell. I've been hiking as fast as I can for the last 45 minutes to catch you. I had to use the toilet back there," I said panting a bit.

We stopped and took a snack break. Skittles caught up and laughed at both of us as he had figured out what was going on. Most hikers will leave a trekking pole or some other sign on the trail to let their partners know they've retreated into the bushes to go poop. I had taken to not doing that after a bear almost happened upon my backpack that I had left trailside one time in Montana while going to dig a cathole. I narrowly made it back to my pack in time to keep the bear from shredding it. We decided from then on to either hike together or leave a trekking pole on the side of the trail as a bathroom signal.

~~~

The past few years P.O.D. and I have been doing separate long-distance hikes. It's happened more out of circumstance than preference. As a schoolteacher, she gets summers off. As a forester, summers are my busy season. I tend to have free time to go hiking on the desert trails in the Southwest in early spring and late fall. 2014 saw me hike the 800-mile Grand Enchantment Trail in Arizona and New Mexico. Last year I hiked the 800-mile Arizona Trail over six weeks, split between March and late October. I've really come to love the desert and hiking in warm weather while it's still winter here in Colorado.

P.O.D. hiked the Sierra High Route a few years ago with a couple of friends. It was mid-summer and I couldn't go. It's a really tough and technical route that doesn't spend much time on existing trails. It was P.O.D.'s first multi-week hike since doing long hikes before we met and she came back a new person. Her confidence levels were out the roof as she had almost daily been faced with sketchy traverses on exposed rock ledges and outcroppings all off trail in a remote section of the Sierra. She had received a crash course in advanced-level hiking and navigating. As a result, I found myself leaning on her expertise when she and I tackled the Wind River High Route in Wyoming a few summers ago. Our roles had completely reversed since those early days on the Continental Divide Trail. All you male hikers out there who think that you know everything about hiking and leading the way, put your egos aside and realize your significant others might just know a thing or two more.

~~~

It's always the most beautiful photos from a long hike that we show our friends and families. It makes them think that the multi-month journey we just completed is all butterflies, rainbows and marital bliss. How romantic that we got to share a four-month adventure together, right?

The truth is that most people don't take photos of their worst moments on trail. You don't see images of two hikers walking together silently, too mad at each other to speak. Or images of two hikers standing in a meadow shouting curses to the heavens, baffled as to where the trail is, swatting mosquitoes and wishing they were anywhere but there. But the true romance is when those two hikers are wet, dirty, exhausted, and smelly and choose to say a kind word or exchange a hug. It's so easy not to do those things when hiking with your significant other, when you are hanging on by a thread and at a breaking point. P.O.D. is much better at this sort of thing than I am, but I strive to get better at it on every hike we take on. I am grateful for every day we get to spend on trail together, even the days when we don't take photos.

~ Epilogue ~

Shortly after I finished writing the draft of this book, P.O.D. and I drove south to begin a month-long ramble of an obscure hiking route in northern New Mexico. We had suffered a particularly dry winter here in southern Colorado and New Mexico was even worse off. The dry winter had snowballed into a rather horrendous spring allergy season which I was unable to escape. All of the usual stuff I do for typically mild seasonal allergies was not working in the spring of 2018. I just kept telling myself not to worry about it and to get to the trail and everything would work itself out.

I'd been feeling woozy for the better part of a month and that feeling did not magically disappear on the first day of our hike in New Mexico. Within a few hours of setting out on journey, I felt fairly rotten. The route we were on was going to become rather remote rather quickly so I relayed to P.O.D. that something was wrong. We took a break and talked over our options. For only the second time in 15,000+ miles of hiking, I turned back. Apparently the climate and vegetation in northern New Mexico is quite similar to southern Colorado, so any hope that the hike would ease my allergies was a bad bet to say the least.

Our good friends who had dropped us off came back and picked us up. We spent a few days at their house hoping my allergies would calm down. Then we read that the Santa Fe National Forest was closing. Indefinitely. This was a problem as the bulk of our planned hike was in Santa Fe National Forest.

The lack of winter had led to severe drought conditions and extreme fire danger in early June of 2018. The US Forest Service had made the preemptive decision to close all 1.5 million acres of Santa Fe National Forest in hopes of preventing a human-caused catastrophic wildfire. Apparently 70 unattended campfires had been found during the previous weekend on the Sante Fe. 70 unattended campfires left by self-absorbed dumbasses in a national forest that had already been under a fire ban for weeks due to extreme fire danger. I can't blame them for closing the entire national forest.

We drove back to Colorado feeling a bit deflated. Our great plan to spend a month hiking in New Mexico wasn't meant to be and we didn't really have a Plan B. But we did have two sections of the Colorado Trail that we maintain that we had yet to set foot on that year. So we switched gears rather quickly and spent a solid two weeks clearing 100+ trees that had fallen across the 16 miles of trail we were in charge of. We cut back an untold amount of willows where our trail skirted high alpine lakes and spent most of our days outside making the best of our "failed" 2018 hike. We were even able to provide some "trail magic" to early season Continental Divide Trail northbound thru-hikers in the form of "wheat sodas."

It won't be long, though, before we head back out there again. If you see us out there, say hello. And by all means don't forget how lucky you are to be on trail. Cheers!

~ Acknowledgements ~

There are more than a few people that I owe a debt of gratitude to in the making of this book. I'd like to thank the initial reviewers of the early drafts: Mark Hyams, Richard Larson, Liz Thomas, Glen Van Peski, Felicia Hermosillo, Eric Payne, Rebecca Taylor, and my parents.

I'd like to thank the following folks for providing blurbs for the book: Philip Connors, M. John Fayhee, Shawn Forry, Michael Gurnow, Rachel Levin, and Liz Thomas.

A special debt of gratitude goes to Cam Honan for writing the Foreword for this book and for sharing some tequila.

Thanks to Leslie Henslee for the cover design and a pot of gold.

Thanks go to Jon Krakauer whose book *Eiger Dreams* provided the inspiration to create two books of short stories about long-distance hiking.

Thanks and praise goes to the Jon Spencer Blues Explosion whose music has helped power me up countless long climbs and put an extra pep in my step when the days got long.

A big thanks goes to all the trail organizations and trail maintainers out there who spend countless hours toiling both in the dirt and behind computers to maintain some of the most incredible trails on our planet!

Thanks goes to all the folks whom I've been fortunate enough to share a trail with. Invariably you all made my hikes more enjoyable and memorable.

To my wife and best friend, Felicia a.k.a. P.O.D., your companionship on what is now 7,000+ miles of hiking is something I value more than I'll ever be able to put into words. I promise to learn Spanish soon!

And finally once again, to the trails and the great people that hike them, this book would not have been possible without the company of both.

Lawton Grinter is an author, forester, trail runner, podcaster and veteran long-distance hiker having completed end-to-end hikes of the Appalachian Trail, Continental Divide Trail and two hikes of the Pacific Crest Trail. In addition to the "Big 3" he has also hiked the John Muir Trail, Colorado Trail, Grand Enchantment Trail, Arizona Trail and New Zealand's Te Araroa in his 15,000+ miles of long-distance hiking. His first book, *I Hike,* was a finalist for TGO Outdoor Book of the Year. He lives in Salida, Colorado.

THE TRAIL SHOW

LESS GEAR   MORE BEER

thetrailshow.com

The Trail Show podcast is a monthly mash-up of all things trail. The Trail Show's reach is international, having been downloaded in 150+ countries since its inception in 2012, yet its focus remains on hiking culture and long-distance hiking trails in the US. Give The Trail Show a listen today and by all means....

Get On The Trail!

www.ingramcontent.com/pod-product-compliance
Lightning Source LLC
LaVergne TN
LVHW091214080426
835509LV00009B/988